EXCEPTIONALITY, *11*(1), 1–2

T0353050

PREFACE

Message From the Guest Editors:
An Introduction to the Special Issue—Part II

Marcia L. Rock and Edwin S. Ellis

Department of Interdisciplinary Teacher Education
University of Alabama

As we posited in Part I of this special issue, time is an important consideration for teachers to address when they are teaching students how to acquire, maintain, and generalize strategic approaches to learning. Time also poses a quandary to the educators who are attempting to promote the use of strategy instruction in classroom settings. Teachers are the engines that drive the delivery of strategic instructional approaches to students who need them. Rarely is time allocated for teachers to interact with one another within the framework of collaborative consultation. Like the gridlock that plagues metropolitan areas during rush hour, "timelock" interferes with the efficacy of collaborative consultation processes (Dettmer, Dyck, & Thurston, 1999; Keyes, 1991). The time that general and special education teachers need to collaboratively prepare and plan for the provision of strategic approaches to instruction is simply not available during the school day.

Part II of this special issue of *Exceptionality* features three articles that are also timely and relevant to the topic of strategic instruction. Boudah, Blair, and Mitchell explore the issue of traversing the research-to-practice abyss through the implementation of authentic and effective professional development. Boudah et al. remind us that "business as usual" approaches to teacher in-service programs are unlikely to produce meaningful changes in teachers' classroom practices.

The remaining two articles offer strategic instructional approaches to facilitate students' learning. Smolkin and Donovan advocate the use of the interactive information book read-aloud methodology to support comprehension acquisition by emerging and struggling readers in the primary grades. These authors provide support for this approach by offering examples of student responses from their research endeavors, and they conclude that this technique seems to be effective in engaging young male students who are often alienated by traditional story-type texts.

Butler's article focuses on structuring instruction to promote self-regulated learning. She begins by delineating the theoretical and empirical basis for the strategic content learning (SCL) model and proceeds with a description of her naturalistic, multischool investigation of SCL with adolescent and adult learners with learning disabilities.

Parts I and II of this topical issue of *Exceptionality* are aimed at improving not only the strategic approaches employed by students with learning disabilities, but also those employed by their teachers and the educational researchers who influence the field of practice. Combined, the authors review the existing literature in varied ways to offer theoretical and empirical frameworks for enhancing strategic approaches to teaching and learning. Each article raises important questions about existing practices and offers innovative alternatives for improving outcomes for students and teachers. The time has arrived for a new vision and a renewed commitment to promoting strategic approaches to learning across and within the educational community.

REFERENCES

Dettmer, P., Dyck, N., & Thurston, L. P. (1999). *Consultation, collaboration, and teamwork for students with special needs* (3rd ed.). Needham Heights, MA: Allyn & Bacon.

Keyes, R. (1991). *Timelock: How life got so hectic and what you can do about it.* New York: Academic.

ARTICLES

Implementing and Sustaining Strategies Instruction: Authentic and Effective Professional Development or "Business as Usual"?

Daniel J. Boudah

School of Education
University of North Carolina at Chapel Hill

Ellen Blair

Bryan Independent School District
Bryan, Texas

Vickie J. Mitchell

Region IV Educational Service Center
Houston, Texas

Professional development that affects teacher practices and student performance does not imply simple, short-term, 1-way solutions, or "business as usual." Professional development that is well matched to teacher needs may be acutely important in enabling in-service teachers to teach academically diverse classes that include students with learning disabilities. Thus, the authentic professional development (APD) model was created and implemented as an effective approach for providing authentic, or teacher-friendly, professional development, particularly for the use of instructional and learning strategies from the strategies instructional model (e.g., Deshler & Schumaker, 1988). Teachers in the experimental group participated in the APD model at their schools, whereas comparison teachers participated in traditional professional development at a separate location. In this article, we describe the APD model and detail the results of a quantitative and qualitative study

Requests for reprints should be sent to Daniel J. Boudah, School of Education, University of North Carolina, 101 Peabody Hall, Chapel Hill, NC 27599-3500. E-mail: boudah@email.unc.edu investigating the impact of APD on teacher use, perceived student outcomes, and teacher value.

Much is known about the effectiveness of strategies instruction for improving the outcomes of students with and without disabilities (cf. other articles in this issue). This convincing database suggests that teachers should teach students how to learn as well as what to learn and should enhance rather than water down the content for students in inclusive classes. These conclusions are illustrated most powerfully through the more than 20-year history of work conducted by researchers from and collaborators with the University of Kansas Center for Research on Learning. From their work, the strategies instructional model (SIM) was initiated and led to the validation of the learning strategies curriculum (e.g., Deshler & Schumaker, 1988) as well as the content enhancement routines (e.g., Bulgren & Lenz, 1996). The learning strategies curriculum includes a number of research-validated learning strategies for students to use independently, and the content enhancement routines are instructional strategies for teachers to use in content-area classes. Together, the strategies and routines provide a strong repertoire of tools for teaching students with and without disabilities to read, write, organize, understand, remember, and express information more effectively.

The content enhancement routines are particularly well suited for implementation by content-area teachers who teach students with learning disabilities (LD) and other disabilities in inclusive classes. As with many poor-performing students, students with LD bring a number of weaknesses to classrooms and often exhibit large deficits in academic achievement (e.g., Deshler, Schumaker, Alley, Warner, & Clark, 1982). Along with their peers, particularly at the high school level, these students are confronted with content that often contains many complex ideas, is poorly organized, and taxes students' ability to remember numerous details (e.g., Schumaker & Deshler, 1984). Given such obstacles, the fact that a large proportion of these and other at-risk adolescents drop out of school is not surprising (U.S. Department of Education, 2000).

In response to classroom demands and student needs, content enhancement routines engage teachers in (a) making planning decisions about what critical content to emphasize in teaching, (b) transforming the content into learner-friendly formats, and (c) presenting science, social studies, or other content to academically diverse groups of students in memorable ways. In short, through application of sound instructional principles and techniques, all students' learning is enriched without sacrifice of important content, and instruction is carried out in an engaging partnership with students.

A number of content enhancement instructional strategies were developed and validated in cooperation with teachers (e.g., Bulgren, Schumaker, & Deshler, 1988, 1994) and were further translated into teacher products that are commercially available with training. One content enhancement routine is called the *unit organizer routine* (Boudah, Lenz, Bulgren, Schumaker, & Deshler, 2000; Lenz, Bulgren, Schumaker, Deshler, & Boudah, 1994). The unit organizer routine is used to help teachers plan for, introduce, and build a unit so that all students can (a) understand how the unit is part of larger course ideas or a sequence of units; (b) understand the gist, or central idea, of the unit through a meaningful paraphrase of the unit title;

(c) see the structure or the organization of the critical unit information; (d) define the relationships associated with the critical information; (e) generate and answer questions about key unit information; (f) monitor progress and accomplishments in learning; and (g) keep the main ideas and the structure of the unit in mind as the unit content is learned. In this study, teachers and administrators chose to learn and implement the unit organizer routine. Figure 1 shows an example of the central instructional device used in this routine.

No matter how high the quality of validated strategies or how well designed the training materials may be, other critical factors influence the implementation and sustainability of research-based strategy instruction in classrooms. Teachers often cite barriers including the inaccessibility of teacher-friendly research reports and a lack of time for reflection on such information (Fullan, 1991; Merriam, 1986). Another important reason that validated practices are uncommon or rarely implemented is the poor match between teacher needs and in-service topics or instructional formats (e.g., Boudah & Mitchell, 1998; Guskey, 1986; Joyce & Showers, 1995). Even the most well-intentioned teacher in-service plans that district administrators make at the beginning of the school year often result in few classroom changes when such plans are operationalized without significant teacher engagement throughout a long-term change process, involvement of key change agents, and essential time and money. As a result, many teachers typically acquire strategies and materials for classroom use by simply walking down the school hall and asking for ideas or activity suggestions from a colleague (Kaestle, 1993).

Furthermore, researchers (Boudah, Logan, & Greenwood, 2001) working on research-to-practice projects, sponsored by the U.S. Department of Education's Office of Special Education Programs, concluded that development, implementation, and sustainability of research-based practices in special education require the following: (a) an up-front commitment by researchers and teachers, as well as an ongoing, honest relationship; (b) intensive work by researchers and teachers; (c) extensive, sustained effort; (d) building-level (although not necessarily district-level) administrative support; (e) the involvement of key individuals; and (f) financial resources and teacher recognition. These researchers' "lessons learned" were similar to those that Schumm and Vaughn (1995) suggested.

Therefore, a critical need exists for increased and improved professional development that has an impact on teacher implementation and sustainability of validated strategies, particularly for addressing the needs of academically diverse classes that include students considered at risk for failure and mainstreamed students with LD. The purpose of this project was threefold: to develop and implement a successful alternative in-service professional development model for teachers, to facilitate the use of research-based instructional strategies in classroom practice by using the model, and to measure the impact on teacher performance and satisfaction as well as student academic outcomes.

AUTHENTIC PROFESSIONAL DEVELOPMENT MODEL

The authentic professional development (APD) model was initially developed to provide an effective professional development approach for teachers, particularly for implementing instructional and learning strategies from the SIM. The APD model was

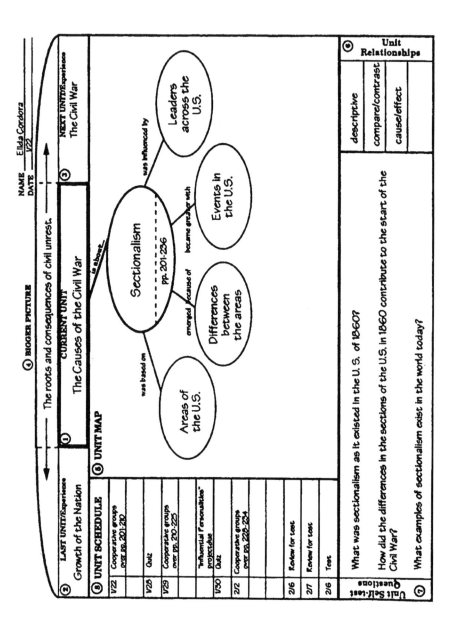

FIGURE 1   The unit organizer.

based on four principles that were translated into a set of specific staff development activities used to address instructional challenges in academically diverse classrooms. According to the APD model, authentic and effective professional development is characterized by (a) quality instruction for adult learners, (b) teacher empowerment, (c) well-matched needs and activities, and (d) sustainable improvements in instruction.

First, the APD model is characterized by the element of quality instruction for adult learners. Adult learners require clear objectives, explicit instruction of theory and skill procedures, observation of demonstrations of practice, individual practice, and feedback so that they can learn effectively and incorporate new skills (Loucks-Horsley et al., 1987; National Partnership for Excellence and Accountability in Teaching [NPEAT], 2000).

Second, the APD model includes teachers as active participants in setting the agenda for the change process, which thereby empowers them to change instructional practices (Hunsaker & Johnston, 1992; Snyder, Bolin, & Zumwalt, 1992). Hence, according to Meyerson (1993), "an educational innovation will be successful when it is viewed by teachers as introspective evolution rather than dictated revolution" (p. 165).

Third, staff development processes and activities must match the needs of stakeholders. All training is aimed at current, relevant problems and issues that teachers are facing within the classes that they teach (Bradley & West, 1994). By addressing real instructional problems in actual classroom settings, the staff development process itself, as well as the instructional strategies implemented, becomes educationally realistic, valid, and useful (Fullan, 1991).

Fourth, by incorporating specific and individualized teacher follow-up, the instructional changes are likely to be more sustainable. Collegial support and follow-up are conducted by knowledgeable colleagues, who provide coaching to teachers as they implement and refine instructional interventions (e.g., Fullan & Hargreaves, 1996; Joyce & Showers, 1995).

SETTING AND PARTICIPANTS

This study occurred in a school district in the U.S. South–Southwest. The 350-square-mile district serves more than 28,000 students and is growing at a rate of 5% annually. The district employs more than 2,000 professional staff members who serve a diverse student population residing in rural areas as well as in planned communities. In recent years, the district has increased its emphasis on including students with disabilities in general education classes for instructional services. Concurrently, the State Education Agency also reduced the number of staff development days to 1.5 per year. Teachers must attain additional staff development by using personal time.

This study comprised two parts: an experimental (quantitative) part and a model evaluation (qualitative) part. The experimental part of the study involved 57 teachers who participated in one of two forms of staff development training on the same instructional strategy and completed the Implementation and Student Performance Questionnaire (see Appendix A). The experimental group received APD training, and the comparison, or control, group received traditional training. Forty-four teachers participated in the experimental group, and 13 participated in the comparison, or control, group.

All 44 teachers in the experimental group were female; 88.1% were content-area teachers and 11.9% were special education teachers. Teaching experience ranged from 2 to 30 years (M = 12.73 years). Of the teachers surveyed, 66.7% held bachelor's degrees, 2.4% held bachelor's degrees with additional college credit hours completed, 26.2% held master's degrees, and 4.8% held master's degrees with additional college credit hours completed. Each teacher taught in one of four (three intermediate and one elementary) participating schools.

Of the 13 teachers in the comparison group, approximately 75% were female and 25% were male (1 teacher did not respond); 38.5% were content-area teachers and 61.5% were special education teachers. Teaching experience ranged from 1 to 25 years (M = 14.08 years). Approximately half the comparison group held bachelor's degrees, no one reported having a bachelor's degree with additional college credit hours completed, about one third held master's degrees, and 16.7% held master's degrees with additional college credit hours completed. Each teacher taught in one of eight (elementary through senior high) schools.

In the model evaluation (qualitative) part of the study, 64 teachers and 4 administrators completed the Training Evaluation Questionnaire (see Appendix B). Because this sample was drawn from the same population of educators as the experimental group was, demographic characteristics were deemed similar and are not reported separately. Table 1 provides a summary of participant numbers in the study.

METHOD

Procedures

On the basis of APD model principles, four specific staff development activities were designed: (a) defining instructional problems, targeting strategy solutions, and addressing training logistics; (b) teacher instruction and classroom modeling; (c) teacher practice with observation and feedback; and (d) teacher follow-up and instructional enhancement.

Defining instructional problems, targeting strategy solutions, and addressing training logistics. First, teachers in the experimental group and their building administrators voluntarily met to collaboratively define instructional problem areas and to target one SIM instructional strategy for training (all chose the unit organizer routine).

TABLE 1
Summary of Participant Numbers

| Group | Experimental Study | | Model Evaluation Study | |
	Original Sample	Final Sample	Original Sample	Final Sample
Experimental	66	44		
Comparison	30	13		
Total	96	57	70	68

From there, teachers and administrators addressed on-site scheduling and other logistics for the planned training and classroom demonstrations.

Teacher instruction and classroom modeling. One to 2 weeks later, teachers signed up, participated in 1.5 to 2 hr of on-site training, and observed the trainer modeling or demonstrating implementation of the unit organizer routine in various content-area classrooms with students. At the end of that school day, teachers also debriefed with the trainer about what they learned and observed.

Teacher practice with observation and feedback. During the following week or two, teachers planned their own implementation of the unit organizer routine. The trainer then returned and observed teachers practicing the use of the instructional strategy in which they had been trained. In after-school meetings, the trainer provided group and individual feedback to teachers about their implementation.

Teacher follow-up and instructional enhancement. After several weeks, teachers met again with the trainer individually and in small groups to share successes, to troubleshoot problems, and to create necessary instructional modifications. Additional follow-up meetings were held at the beginning of the following school year.

The APD model was implemented at four school sites, for 3 to 5 weeks at each site, excluding follow-up visits. Initial training was conducted from January through April. Teachers spent approximately 2 hr on the first activity: defining instructional problems and targeting solutions. School principals and administrators then spent approximately 2 additional hr addressing training logistics and making site arrangements. For the second activity, teachers spent 1.5 to 2 hr in training, an additional 1 to 2 hr observing modeling or demonstrations, and approximately 1 hr debriefing. Teacher observation with feedback, the third activity, required teachers to spend 1 to 3 hr of instructional preparation time, at least one class period of instruction while under observation by the trainer, and then approximately 1 hr for debriefing. Time spent on the fourth activity—follow-up and instructional enhancement—varied among individual teachers (1–4 hr) and may have included e-mail correspondence or telephone conversations, face-to-face discussions, and individual instructional modifications during instructional preparation.

The comparison teachers participated in traditional, single-day staff development at a separate school location for 5.5 hr. The training consisted of a description of the instructional strategy and how it can be used but did not include in-class modeling, teacher practice with observation, feedback, or follow-up. These teachers were trained in two groups, in February and March, respectively. All teachers in both groups learned the same SIM instructional strategy procedures—the unit organizer routine (Boudah et al., 2000; Lenz et al., 1994).

Data Collection

In this study, primary data were collected from two sources: (a) the teacher Implementation and Student Performance Questionnaire (see Appendix A) and (b) the teacher Training

Evaluation Questionnaire (see Appendix B). Secondarily, for teacher feedback and for implementation verification purposes, observational data were collected in the classrooms of teachers in the experimental group who participated in the APD model training. Descriptive field notes on instructional performance were collected during observations and used in formative feedback to teachers.

Implementation and Student Performance Questionnaire. At the end of the school year, and according to procedures outlined by Berdie, Anderson, and Niebuhr (1986), a 20-item written questionnaire was mailed to each teacher in the experimental and comparison groups. Teachers responded to multiple-choice, yes–no, ranking, and open-ended questions about implementation of the unit organizer routine, perceived changes in student performance as a result of using this routine, and satisfaction with the routine. Teachers responded to questionnaire items about student performance by using data that they gathered in their classrooms. These data included quarterly and semester grades, unit test and quiz scores, assignment completion rates, and classroom engagement rates. (See Appendix A for the questionnaire.)

The questionnaire was mailed to 96 teachers—66 in the experimental group and 30 in the comparison group. Forty-four of the 66 teachers in the experimental group returned their surveys (return rate, 66.67%). Thirteen of the 30 teachers in the comparison group returned their surveys (return rate, 43.33%). The total return rate across both groups was 59.38%.

Training Evaluation Questionnaire. After the training, demonstrations, teacher observations, and initial follow-up meetings with teachers, a written questionnaire was distributed to teachers and administrators during meetings at schools at which the APD model had been implemented. Six open-ended questions were designed to garner multiple participant perspectives on the characteristics of the model that participants deemed effective. The questions addressed the parts of APD that were most valued and those that were not, the advantages and disadvantages of APD over traditional staff development, and whether teachers would recommend this type of training approach. (See Appendix B for the questionnaire.) Sixty-eight of 70 teachers and administrators completed the surveys (return rate, 97.14%).

Data Analysis

Implementation and Student Performance Questionnaire. Descriptive and statistical analyses were conducted on various multiple-choice, yes–no, and ranking item responses from the Implementation and Student Performance Questionnaire. Responses from open-ended questions on the survey were also noted. Mean implementation rates were statistically analyzed for differences between the experimental group and the comparison group by using analysis of variance (ANOVA) procedures employing the experimental group as the two-level independent factor (Borg & Gall, 1983). Descriptive statistics (frequencies, percentages, frequency ranges) were computed for item responses regarding extent of implementation, characteristics of teacher implementation, interest in further SIM training, and perceived changes in student performance. As a way to analyze the differences in implementation between the experimental and comparison groups, differential trainer effects were controlled by using the same trainer or staff development presenter for the experimental and comparison groups.

Training Evaluation Questionnaire.   A consultant external to the study analyzed responses to the Training Evaluation Questionnaire, in stages consistent with the principles of naturalistic unitizing and categorizing (Lincoln & Guba, 1985). As a result of the consultant's peripheral involvement with the project, the examination of the data was independent and nonbiased.

The first phase of analysis consisted of coding each response on each teacher's returned questionnaire. The codes indicated the month and location of the APD workshop, the respondent number, and the question number. The coded responses were cut apart with scissors; hand sorted by question; examined for evidence of quality, content, usefulness, and applicability of the model; and reexamined for convergence and divergence of replies. A comprehensive listing of all written responses was created. The slips of paper, representing individual participant response units, were then grouped according to tentative categories or themes and by survey question number. The frequency of responses was tallied within and across the six questions. Through this process, four categories were identified. For each of the six questions, tables were created to reflect the tentative categories or themes and the responses that emerged from the initial analysis.

The second phase began with grouping participant response statements that reflected positive regard for the APD model separate from those that reflected negative regard for the APD model. Each unit of data (i.e., written response) was then transposed to a 3- by 5-in. note card with a category or theme name from the initial analysis written on it. Some revisions took place at this stage, but four major categories or themes were retained from the data: setting, timing, format, and content. The frequencies of positive and negative responses by category or theme were then calculated, regardless of question number. Response percentages were also calculated when meaningful. Tables were then created to reflect the positive and negative response statements, and their frequency, by each of the four major categories of responses.

RESULTS

Implementation and Student Performance Questionnaire

We briefly described the results of the analysis of implementation rates of the experimental and comparison teachers, as well as findings regarding perceived changes in student performance, elsewhere (Boudah & Mitchell, 1998). However, in summary, 42 (95%) of 44 teachers who participated in APD model training and responded to the questionnaire reported that they had implemented the unit organizer routine in which they had been trained, with a range of 91% to 100% across the four participating schools. Only 5 (38%)

of 13 responding teachers who participated in traditional in-service training reported that they had implemented the unit organizer routine after training. On the basis of the ANOVA, the difference was statistically significant, $F(2, 51) = 55.587, p < .0001$. As a way to verify questionnaire responses about implementation, 53 of 66 teachers who participated in the APD model training were also observed implementing the unit organizer routine that they were taught to use. Teachers in the comparison (traditional in-service) group were not observed because of the low probability of implementation based on survey responses.

Moreover, regarding the extent of implementation, 16 of the 42 teachers reportedly used the unit organizer routine more than once during the 1 to 3 months after training—or 36.4% of the 44 experimental teachers, compared with 8.3% of the comparison teachers. Because of such significant differences, the descriptive analysis focused only on responses from the experimental teachers.

The teachers in the experimental group were asked to detail how student performance was affected by implementation of the unit organizer routine. Choosing from a list of possible responses (including class assignments, homework grades, projects, test scores, and other student performance indicators), 75% of the responding teachers said that overall student engagement rates had improved and 53% said that in-class assignments had improved. In addition, 28% of the teachers thought that overall test scores had been affected by use of the strategy. Specifically regarding perceived changes in the performance of students who were low achieving and those with LD, teachers most often noted improved engagement rates (62%) and improved performance on in-class assignments (35%). Eighteen percent of responding teachers also thought that the test scores of students who were low achieving and those with LD had been affected by implementing the strategy.

Of the teachers involved in APD model training, 53.7% reportedly modified or adapted the unit organizer routine to better accommodate the needs of students with LD. Table 2 provides a summary of the percentage of responses to the questionnaire.

TABLE 2
Responses to the Implementation and Student Performance Questionnaire

Item	Experimental Group (%)	Comparison Group (%)
Implemented unit organizer	95.0	38.0
Used unit organizer more than once	36.4	8.3
Overall student engagement improved	75.0	
Overall in-class assignments improved	53.0	
Overall test scores improved	28.0	
LD and LA student engagement improved	62.0	
LD and LA in-class assignments improved	35.0	
LD and LA test scores improved	18.0	
Created modifications	53.7	

Note. LD = learning disabled; LA = low achieving.

Training Evaluation Questionnaire

Foremost, more than 80% of the participants' responses to the Training Evaluation Questionnaire were positive and supportive of the APD model. Respondents were particularly enthusiastic about the opportunity to observe classroom modeling of unit organizer implementation as a part of the training. Moreover, participants seemed to value observing the process on their home campuses and in their own classrooms. The "hands-on" involvement of the trainer in "real classroom" environments with "real students" was cited most often as an APD model asset. In addition, teachers liked the convenience of participating in the training during the regular school day and not enduring the additional burden of preparing for a substitute teacher. Table 3 summarizes the responses in support of the APD model.

Approximately 20% of the comments that participants made were directed toward areas in need of improvement. The logistics of arranging for one teacher to cover two classes to facilitate release time for another to observe the trainer's classroom demonstration proved difficult for some. Others found the schedule hectic and stressful. Table 4 summarizes the responses referencing aspects of the training model in need of attention.

Question 1 of the questionnaire asked, "What did you like about having this training in your building?" More than half the teacher responses related to the category or

TABLE 3
Training Evaluation Questionnaire: Positive Responses

Category	Positive Responses	No. Responses
Setting	Convenience in the building	68
	Small groups; more personal	3
Timing	Timing during the school/work day	20
Format	Modeling/observation with own students	86
	No subs; class schedule can be adjusted	17
	Immediate/specific feedback	12
	Opportunity to try something new	8
	Comfortable; provided peer support	5
	Excellent use of time	4
	Opportunity to practice	3
	Collaborative	2
	Return to students quickly	2
	Teachers visiting other classrooms	1
	Organization	1
	Peer relationships strengthened	1
Content	Use of unit organizers	9
	Relevant and responsive to needs	6
	Videos/books/handouts	5
	Unique to school	4
	Only essential parts taught	1
Other	Informative; gave the big picture	5
	Helped develop ownership	1

TABLE 4
Training Evaluation Questionnaire: Negative Responses

Category	Needs Attention	No. Responses
Setting	On campus does not provide mental break	1
Timing	Hectic schedule; rushed/stressed	9
	Too close to TAAS	6
	Required to meet at lunch or after school	6
	Time away from students	5
	Content mastery had to be closed	1
Format	One teacher covering two classes	10
	Need more time to practice and prepare	5
	Not available to all faculty	4
	Too rushed; need more time for sharing	2
	Bells ringing/people moving between classes	1
	Having to be in different places	1
Content	Needs more observation/modeling	6
	More preparation required	3
	Visual overload; too many overheads	2
	Clearer handouts needed	1

Note. TAAS = Texas Assessment of Academic Skills.

theme of setting, particularly to the value of having the training conducted in their own buildings. More than half the respondents also liked the format—a second category of responses—particularly the opportunity to observe the instructional strategy demonstration with their own students. For example, one teacher wrote this: "The unit organizer is a valuable organizing and teaching tool for teachers and students. Being able to see it modeled, then having the opportunity to try it out with students and be critiqued by an 'expert' is so valuable."

In Question 2, teachers were asked, "What parts of how this was done would you keep?" Twenty-eight responses again related to the format of training, particularly the classroom instructional modeling or demonstration with students. In response to this question, one teacher noted, "[I would keep] All parts—the morning presentation time was good, visiting classrooms/observing was helpful, afternoon debriefing time—great." Nearly half of the respondents wrote that they would keep all activities included in the APD model implementation.

As a way to confirm participants' responses to the previous question, Question 3 requested information on any negative aspects of the model that need to be eliminated. The majority of respondents (40 of 68) indicated that none of the model's elements should be "thrown away," and 15 offered no response. Among the 13 remaining respondents, 6 teachers noted timing, particularly insufficient time to plan and meet for feedback.

Question 4 was an additional attempt to garner information about potential areas needing improvement. Most respondents recommended making no substantial changes to the APD model or simply left the question response section blank. Six teachers commented on format, which suggests that teachers have more opportunities to observe instructional demonstrations, and a smaller number said that more time for preparation and practice would have been helpful.

Question 5 was a two-part question asking about the advantages and disadvantages of the APD model. Forty-five respondents again noted the value of instructional modeling in the real-world environment of the classroom and in addressing actual instructional issues. More than half the teachers either indicated that there were no disadvantages or simply left the question response section blank. Teachers offered a handful of disadvantages directed at timing, primarily the limited amount of time available for the initial training and, as a consequence, the compact schedule. For example, for the advantages, one teacher wrote, "Involved real classroom" and for disadvantages, the same teacher wrote, "Took time away from day (although you/I/we can't have it both ways)."

In Question 6, the researchers were interested in knowing if the participants would recommend this type of nontraditional staff development to teachers at other school campuses, and if so, why? Sixty-five (96%) of 68 respondents answered "yes." Again, classroom demonstration or modeling emerged as a consistent reason, as did practicality, relevance, and convenience.

DISCUSSION

One goal of this project was to design, implement, and evaluate the effects of the APD model on teacher implementation and perceived student performance in one school district. A second goal was to assess teacher perceptions of the components of the model, both in general and in specific. Overall, much higher teacher implementation rates were reported and observed in the classrooms of teachers who participated in the APD model than in classrooms of teachers who participated in traditional staff development. Some aspects of overall student performance reportedly improved in APD model teachers' classrooms, some aspects of the performance of students who were low achieving and those with LD also improved in APD model teachers' classrooms, and most APD teachers reportedly made modifications for students with LD. These results provide some direction in addressing the question "What makes teacher professional development successful?"

Teacher responses on the Training Evaluation Questionnaire provide additional answers to this question. In sum, teachers who participated in the APD model responded positively to the model setting, format, timing, and content. The responses to Question 1 highlighted the strength of on-site training and the instructional format. Responses to Question 2 underscored support for engaging teachers as active learners and enabling teachers to observe new techniques, and further promoted the positive aspects of the demonstration, practice, and feedback. Teacher responses to Question 5 were once more supportive of modeling in the real-world environment of the classroom and in addressing actual instructional issues. Moreover, given that only 20% of all questionnaire responses reflected anything negative (even though in half the questions participants were prompted to indicate areas needing improvement) and that nearly 100% of the respondents said that they would recommend the APD model to colleagues, the model appears to have some credibility.

Limitations

The generalizability of the results to other schools and teachers may be limited in several ways. First, the data set largely consists of teacher self-report data, and if measured otherwise, teacher and student performances may have been different than those reported by the teachers. Second, the generalizability of these results is also limited to teachers who returned surveys, even though most of the implementation responses by teachers in the experimental group on the Implementation and Student Performance Questionnaire were verified. Still, the sample is relatively small, and we do not know whether the performances or perceptions of the responding teachers differed from those of teachers who did not return the questionnaire or would differ from those of teachers in other locations. Thus, the sample error rate was calculated as 13% on the basis of the overall sample of 57 respondents. Third, because of the unequal size of the participant groups in the experimental design, results from that part of the study may be problematic. Fourth, results from the study may also have limited generalizability because the reliability and the validity of the questionnaires were not statistically determined.

Implications

Nevertheless, the APD model holds promise for becoming a successful vehicle for professional development in school settings, and it may be adapted for use by other school districts with similar needs but different resources. However, future APD model implementation would be enhanced by initiation earlier in the school year and include more time for apprenticeship-like coaching in teacher follow-up activities. Evaluation should also include objective measures of teacher and student performance rather than relying on teacher self-reports, particularly for making important assessments of the progress of students with LD. Such efforts, as well as additional studies using other SIM learning strategies or content enhancement routines with teachers in other school systems, may shed further light on the APD model and other models that attempt to create authentic and effective professional development.

Furthermore, the APD model is perhaps only an approximation of what it is required to ensure successful implementation and sustainability of learning strategies instruction or content enhancement routines. On the basis of this study, as well as other work (e.g., Boudah et al., 2001; Fuchs & Fuchs, 1998; Fullan & Hargreaves, 1996; Joyce & Showers, 1995; NPEAT, 2000; Schumm & Vaughn, 1995), four major components to successful professional development of teachers are apparent: (a) student-oriented goals and outcomes, (b) data-driven and teacher-friendly processes, (c) quality content for teacher use, and (d) essential supports from inside and outside the school.

Student-oriented goals and outcomes.   School services, in general, and professional development, in specific, should have a student-oriented focus with regard to strategies instruction (or any other intervention). Further, the goals of school services and professional development activities should be geared toward increasing student performance (e.g., Fullan & Hargreaves, 1996; Joyce & Showers, 1995). So that such goals can be accomplished, professional development plans and activities should focus on enhancing and remediating (when necessary) the performance of students with and without disabilities. The effort represented in this study is consistent with this point in that although the APD model was designed to directly affect teacher performance, students were the ultimate recipients of benefits.

Data-driven and teacher-friendly processes.   Instructional and professional development decisions should be data driven and teacher friendly as well (e.g., Fullan, 1991; Joyce & Showers, 1995; NPEAT, 2000). Being data driven, particularly for special educators, should not be a foreign idea; after all, individualized education plans are intended to be data-driven, live documents based on student strengths and weaknesses as measured in multiple ways. Teacher strengths and needs, as well as professional development activities, should also be addressed through ongoing evaluation. In addition, just as students receiving special education services are entitled to individualized services, teachers should be provided with individualized, apprenticeship-like opportunities that include voice in training decisions, intensive instruction on potent instructional strategies, opportunities to watch real-time classroom demonstrations, collaborative dialogue to troubleshoot interventions with colleagues, and coaching. In this study, teachers apparently valued such opportunities in the training process.

Quality content for teacher use.   Clearly, teachers also need quality content in professional development activities. A quality process without meaningful content is like a fine automobile without gasoline. Teachers need to develop skillful knowledge about and receive teacher-friendly materials for implementing research-validated strategies (Boudah et al., 2001; NPEAT, 2000). In this study, teachers were introduced to and then implemented the unit organizer routine, a research-tested and useful focus for professional learning (Boudah et al., 2000; Lenz et al., 1994). According to the results from the Training Evaluation Questionnaire, teachers seemed to view the routine as quality professional development content.

Essential supports from inside and outside the school.   Increasing the capacity for teachers to learn, implement, and sustain the use of research-based strategy interventions demands critical support from building administrators and knowledgeable outsiders such as university educators (e.g., Boudah et al., 2001; Schumm & Vaughn, 1995). School administrators and building principals need to provide funding for materials and training, and, perhaps more important, the time for teachers to collaboratively define instructional problem areas, target training needs, create and learn about research-based interventions, collect meaningful data, and evaluate student and professional development outcomes. University educators and other professional researchers from rural and urban areas can engage in meaningful and mutually beneficial partnerships with schools by creating formal or informal professional development school (PDS) or PDS-like ties. By doing so, schools can gain valuable access to expertise and ongoing support for integrating strategy instruction into classrooms. In this project, although none of the schools was formally identified as a PDS, the long-term relationship built between the school and the university trainer provided the opportunity for teachers in each experimental school to receive feedback necessary to increase implementation and the likelihood of sustainability of strategy instruction.

Finally, these four components for teacher development have additional legitimacy because comparable concepts were embedded in an agenda for improving teacher professional development that was recently voiced by the NPEAT (2000), a voluntary association of 29 national organizations, including the Council for Exceptional Children. However, use of these components to develop teacher expertise is not necessarily a new idea. Joyce and Showers (1995), as well as other educators, have been advocating many similar ideas for some time. However, to operationalize these four important components to ensure well-implemented and sustainable strategies instruction continues to imply anything but traditional staff development ("business as usual") for schools and educators.

REFERENCES

Berdie, D. R., Anderson, J. F., & Niebuhr, M. A. (1986). *Questionnaires: Design and use.* Metuchen, NJ: Scarecrow.

Borg, W. R., & Gall, M. D. (1983). *Educational research* (4th ed.). New York: Longman.

Boudah, D. J., Lenz, B. K., Bulgren, J. A., Schumaker, J. B., & Deshler, D. D. (2000, January/February). Don't water down! Enhance content learning through the unit organizer routine. *Teaching Exceptional Children, 32*(3), 48–56.

Boudah, D. J., Logan, K. R., & Greenwood, C. R. (2001). The research to practice projects: Lessons learned about changing teacher practice. *Teacher Education and Special Education, 24,* 290–303.

Boudah, D. J., & Mitchell, V. J. (1998). The real thing. *Journal of Staff Development, 19*(3), 43–47.

Bradley, D. F., & West, J. F. (1994). Staff training for the inclusion of students with disabilities: Visions from school-based educators. *Teacher Education and Special Education, 17,* 117–128.

Bulgren, J. A., & Lenz, B. K. (1996). Strategic instruction in the content areas. In D. D. Deshler, E. S. Ellis, & B. K. Lenz (Eds.), *Teaching adolescents with learning disabilities: Strategies and methods* (2nd ed., pp. 409–473). Denver, CO: Love.

Bulgren, J. A., Schumaker, J. B., & Deshler, D. D. (1988). Effectiveness of a concept teaching routine in enhancing the performance of LD students in secondary-level mainstream classes. *Learning Disability Quarterly, 11,* 3–17.

Bulgren, J. A., Schumaker, J. B., & Deshler, D. D. (1994). The effects of a recall enhancement routine on the test performance of secondary students with and without learning disabilities. *Learning Disabilities Research and Practice, 9*(1), 2–11.

Deshler, D. D., & Schumaker, J. B. (1988). An instructional model for teaching students how to learn. In J. L. Graden, J. E. Curtis, & M. J. Curtis (Eds.), *Alternative educational delivery systems: Enhancing instructional options for all students* (pp. 391–441). Washington, DC: National Association of School Psychologists.

Deshler, D. D., Schumaker, J. B., Alley, G. R., Warner, M. M., & Clark, F. L. (1982). Learning disabilities in adolescent and young adult populations: Research implications. *Focus on Exceptional Children, 15,* 1–12.

Fuchs, D., & Fuchs, L. S. (1998). Researchers and teachers working together to adapt instruction for diverse learners. *Learning Disabilities Research and Practice, 13,* 126–137.

Fullan, M. G. (1991). *The new meaning of educational change* (2nd ed.). New York: Teachers College Press.

Fullan, M. G., & Hargreaves, A. (1996). *What's worth fighting for in your school?* New York: Teachers College Press.

Guskey, T. R. (1986). Staff development and the process of teacher change. *Educational Researcher, 15,* 5–12.

Hunsaker, L., & Johnston, M. (1992). Teacher under construction: A collaborative case study of teacher change. *American Educational Research Journal, 29,* 350–372.

Joyce, B., & Showers, B. (1995). *Student achievement through staff development: Fundamentals of school renewal* (2nd ed.). New York: Longman.

Kaestle, C. (1993). The awful reputation of educational research. *Educational Researcher, 22*(1), 23–31.

Lenz, B. K., Bulgren, J. A., Schumaker, J. B., Deshler, D. D., & Boudah, D. J. (1994). *The content enhancement series: The unit organizer routine.* Lawrence, KS: Edge Enterprises.

Lincoln, Y. S., & Guba, E. G. (1985). *Naturalistic inquiry.* Newbury Park, CA: Sage.

Loucks-Horsley, S., Harding, C. K., Arbuckle, M. A., Murray, L. B., Dubea, C., & Williams, M. K. (1987). *Continuing to learn: A guidebook for teacher development.* Andover, MA: Regional Laboratory for Educational Improvement of the Northeast and Islands.

Merriam, S. B. (1986). *The research to practice dilemma.* Columbus, OH: National Center Publications, National Center for Research in Vocational Education. (ERIC Document Reproduction Service No. ED278801)

Meyerson, M. J. (1993). Exploring reading instructional decisions through a reflective activity: A first step in the change process. *Journal of Educational and Psychological Consultation, 4,* 153–168.

National Partnership for Excellence and Accountability in Teaching. (2000). *Revisioning professional development.* Oxford, OH: National Staff Development Council.

Schumaker, J. B., & Deshler, D. D. (1984). Setting demand variables: A major factor in program planning for LD adolescents. *Topics in Language Disorders, 4,* 22–44.

Schumm, J. S., & Vaughn, S. (1995). Meaningful professional development in accommodating students with disabilities: Lessons learned. *Remedial and Special Education, 16,* 344–353.

Snyder, J., Bolin, F., & Zumwalt, K. (1992). Curriculum implementation. In P. W. Jackson (Ed.), *Handbook of research on curriculum* (pp. 402–435). New York: Macmillan.

U.S. Department of Education. (2000). *To assure the free appropriate public education of all children with disabilities: Twentieth annual report to Congress on the implementation of The Individuals With Disabilities Education Act.* Washington, DC: Office of Special Education Programs.

APPENDIX A

Implementation and Student Performance Questionnaire

Thank you for participating in [the district's] new "adventure in staff development" during this school year. Your feedback is vital for evaluating the efficacy of the training approach as well as the content of the training (e.g., unit organizer routine). Please spend a few moments to give your honest feedback and return your completed questionnaire to

_____ by May 17th.

For the following items, among the response choices given, please check your response.

1. I implemented the unit organizer routine:

   _____ with one unit since the training   _____ with three units since the training

   _____ with two units since the training   _____ with more than three units since the training

2. I received training in the month of:

   _____ January   _____ February   _____ March   _____ April

3. The *approximate average* number of days in each unit that I utilized the unit organizer routine (including introducing the unit, using the expanded unit map, and reviewing the unit with the UO) was:

_____ one day   _____ three days   _____ more than five days

_____ two days   _____ four days

4. Did you modify or adapt the unit organizer in any way for classes or students who may be at risk, low achieving, or have disabilities?

_____ Yes   _____ No

5. If you answered yes to item #4, briefly describe your modification:

6. We are ultimately interested in the effects of content enhancement on the academic performance of students. Please characterize the performance of students in classes in which you implemented the unit organizer routine by checking one of the following:

_____ Academic performance for all or nearly all students was generally unaffected.

_____ Academic performance improved for some students.

_____ Academic performance improved for all or nearly all students.

7. If some, nearly all, or all students' academic performance improved, please describe your students' improved performance by checking all the following that apply:

_____ Improved test/quiz scores

_____ Improved grades/quality of in-class assignments

_____ Improved grades/quality of homework assignments

_____ Higher rate of homework completion

_____ Higher rate of classroom engagement/on-task behavior

_____ Improved grades/quality of class projects

_____ Improved grades/quality of small group work

_____ Improvement was evident in other ways (please briefly describe)

_____

8. In particular, did the academic performance of students who are low achieving and those with disabilities improve?

_____ Yes, for some

_____ Yes, for all or nearly all

_____ No, academic performance was generally unaffected

9. If you answered yes to item #8, please describe the improved performance of

students who are low achieving and those with disabilities by checking all the following that apply:

_____ Improved test/quiz scores

_____ Improved grades/quality of in-class assignments

_____ Improved grades/quality of homework assignments

_____ Higher rate of homework completion

_____ Higher rate of classroom engagement/on-task behavior

_____ Improved grades/quality of class projects

_____ Improved grades/quality of small group work

_____ Improvement was evident in other ways (please briefly describe)

_____

Please provide brief responses to the following items.

10. In what subject area(s) did you use the unit organizer?

11. What was (were) the title(s) of the unit(s) for which you used the unit organizer?

12. If you wish, please share any other comments below regarding this year's "adventure in staff development":

Please provide some feedback with regard to your interest in further training.

13. Would you be interested in further training on content enhancement routines?

_____ Yes   _____ No

If yes, please rank in order *up to three* content enhancement routines that you would be most interested in learning more about in the coming year. Write a "1" next to your first choice.

_____ Unit organizer   _____ Concept mastery

_____ Lesson organizer   _____ Concept anchoring

_____ Concept comparison

14. Would you be interested in further training on *collaboration*, including *co-teaching*?

_____ Yes   _____ No

15. Would you be interested in further training on learning strategies?

_____ Yes   _____ No

If yes, please rank in order *up to three* learning strategies that you would be most interested in learning more about in the coming year. Write a "1" next to your first choice.

_____ Paraphrasing   _____ Sentence writing

_____ Visual imagery   _____ Paragraph writing

_____ Word identification   _____ Theme writing

_____ First-letter mnemonics   _____ Error monitoring

_____ Test taking

Please share a little more about you.

16. I am a(n) (check one) general education teacher_____ special education

teacher_____ principal_____ administrator_____

parent_____ student_____ .

If you are a *general education teacher*, what subject(s) do you teach?

_____

If you are a *special education teacher*, check the environment in which you spend *most* of your time with students with disabilities:

_____ Resource room

_____ Content mastery

_____ Self-contained class for subjects including _____

_____ General education class

_____ Other: _____

17. I currently work at a(n) (check one):

_____ elementary school   _____ junior high school

_____ intermediate/middle school   _____ high school

18. How many years, including this year, have you been teaching? _____

19. What is the highest university degree you have earned? _____

20. My gender is _____ female   _____ male.

APPENDIX B

Training Evaluation Questionnaire

School _____ Date _____

1. What did you like about having this training in your building?

2. What parts of how this was done would you keep?

3. What parts of this type of staff development would you throw away?

4. What parts of this staff development would you keep, but do differently? How?

5. What were the advantages and disadvantages of this model of staff development over traditional staff development?
   Advantages:

   Disadvantages:

6. Would you recommend this type/model of nontraditional staff development to colleagues at other buildings? Why?

EXCEPTIONALITY, *11*(1), 25–38

Supporting Comprehension Acquisition for Emerging and Struggling Readers: The Interactive Information Book Read-Aloud

Laura B. Smolkin

Department of Curriculum, Intruction, and Special Education
University of Virginia

Carol A. Donovan

Department of Interdisciplinary Teacher Education
University of Alabama

This article begins with the suggestion that comprehension-related activities need not wait until children are fluently decoding but may be used during a phase that we term *comprehension acquisition*. We turn our attention to the features of the interactive information book read-aloud, an instructional approach we see as supporting both nonreaders and nonfluent readers prior to the introduction of instruction in cognitive and comprehension strategies. Following our presentation of the 4 key features of this approach—interaction, information books, teacher awareness of text features, and time for in-depth readings—we examine the ways in which these read-alouds relate to what Ellis and Wortham (1999) termed a watering up of curriculum for students with special needs.

That the ability to accurately and speedily recognize words accounts for a significant part of the variance in reading comprehension has long been established (e.g., Perfetti, 1985). Given this finding, the logical approach for reading researchers has been to focus heavily on ways to foster phonemic awareness. It has also been reasonable for special education researchers (e.g., Ellis, 1989) to say that if students are unable to fluently decode, instruction in cognitive strategies should be delayed until such reading skills are in place.

However, the results of certain studies suggest that during instructional periods in which students' attention is focused on the relationship between letters and their sounds,

Requests for reprints should be sent to Laura B. Smolkin, Department of Curriculum, Instruction, and Special Education, Curry School of Education, University of Virginia, 230 Ruffner Hall, Charlottesville, VA 22903-4273. E-mail: lbs5z@virginia.edu little gain is made in listening comprehension. For example, Juel and Leavell (1988) noted that although retention in first grade could lead to improved phonological awareness, it did not lead to increased listening comprehension ability. Morrison, Griffith, and Frazier (1996) noted a similar finding: Various comprehension-related skills, such as world knowledge, vocabulary growth, and text structural awareness, do not flourish during periods in which phonological awareness is the stressed instruction.

These findings are important because they remind us that "efficient word recognition seems to be a necessary but not sufficient condition for good comprehension" (Stanovich, 1991, p. 419). In their chapter, van den Broek and Kremer (2000) drew attention to the various reader, textual, and contextual factors that affect success and failure in comprehension. They suggested that beyond skill in decoding, (a) attention and motivation, (b) allocation of cognitive resources to metacognition and reading strategies, (c) inferential and reasoning skills, and (d) background knowledge all play important roles in determining comprehension success. Adequately addressing these other reader characteristics in designing comprehension instruction even for nonreaders is important, because research shows that specific knowledge can compensate for undeveloped reading skills (Adams, Bell, & Perfetti, 1995).

If students are not yet reading or if they are not yet reading fast enough to benefit from cognitive strategy instruction, how are these various reader characteristics beyond decoding skills to be addressed? In this article, we call attention to the interactive information book read-aloud, an instructional approach that we see as supporting both nonreaders and nonfluent readers prior to the introduction of instruction in cognitive and comprehension strategies. We begin by presenting the key components of the interactive information book read-aloud. We then explore the place of these components within the notion of "watering up" a curriculum (Ellis & Wortham, 1999) for students in special education. We conclude this article by contemplating the types of future research that this precomprehension instruction approach suggests.

DEFINING COMPREHENSION ACQUISITION

We define *comprehension acquisition* as an instructional period that precedes actual comprehension strategy instruction (Smolkin & Donovan, 2001, 2002). In using the term *acquisition*, we follow the lead of second-language-acquisition researcher Krashen (1976, 1981), who sought to distinguish between two types of learning that might occur. He referred to the first as *acquisition*; this process takes place through repeated exposures and interactions with others in naturally occurring family and community events. Acquisition occurs on a mostly subconscious level. Krashen simply termed the second type *learning*, which occurs during periods of formal instruction designed to focus children's attention on a particular type of information or action that has been extracted from its context. As we noted elsewhere (Smolkin & Donovan, 2002), this same distinction in cognitive operations can be seen in Salomon and Perkins's (1989) "low" and "high" roads to transfer. Like Krashen's "acquisition," Salomon and Perkins's "low road" is highly context dependent in that repeated practice in "somewhat related and expanding contexts" (p. 120) results in acquiring cognitive strategies. Like Krashen's "learning,"

Salomon and Perkins's "high road" entails abstraction of information from its context to create a rule or a principle that could be mindfully applied at a future point.

Our attention has settled on contextually supported acquisition in large part due to the writings of developmental psychologist Sheldon White. White (1996), in trying to explain the major shifts in children's cognition between the ages of 5 and 7, indicated that children do not appear to gain an absolute reasoning ability. Instead, he explained, they acquire an ability to reason with others as they discover how we are to act and think in particular settings. For us, his key words are *with others* and *in particular settings*; accordingly, we now turn our attention to a particular setting we have been studying.

THE INTERACTIVE INFORMATION BOOK READ-ALOUD

We noted, as did others (e.g., Duke, 2000; Pappas, 1991), that primary classrooms promote the reading of storybooks and neglect the reading of information, or nonfiction, works. Although we love storybooks as much as anyone, we understand that offering early access to the ideas, vocabulary, syntax, and text structures of informational texts helps prepare children for the time in school when the emphasis in reading instruction shifts from learning to read to reading to learn. We believe that this exposure is as important for nonreaders (children identified with learning disabilities and receiving special education services) as it is for emerging readers (children without disabilities who have not yet mastered the print–sound codes). This belief proves particularly important if we accept that context (including book type) is important in developing reasoning abilities.

Following is an excerpt from the transcript of the interactive read-aloud of Tomie de Paola's (1978) *dual-purpose text* (see Donovan & Smolkin, 2002, for a discussion of this term) *The Popcorn Book*. This excerpt and all others appearing in this article were taken from a 2-year study that contrasted read-alouds of both storybooks and information books in first-grade classrooms. (Underlining indicates that text is being read.)

Teacher: In 1612, French explorers saw some Iroquois people popping corn in clay pots. They would fill the pots with hot sand, throw in some popcorn and stir it with a stick. When the corn popped, it came to the top of the sand and made it easy to get.

Child 1: Look at the bowl!

Teacher: Okay, now it's hot enough to add a few kernels.

Child 2: What's a kernel?

Child 3: Like what you pop.

Teacher: It's a seed.

Annie: What if you, like, would you think [of] a popcorn seed? Like a popcorn seed. Could you grow popcorn?

Teacher: Oh, excellent, excellent, question! Let's read and we'll see if this [book] answers that question, and if not, we'll talk about it at the end.

Many of the key elements of interactive information book read-alouds are illustrated in this short excerpt. Each is discussed briefly in the following subsections.

Interaction

According to Dickinson and Smith (1994), read-alouds can support children's developing ability to reason for themselves and with others, if these events actively involve the children in analytic discussions of the book being read. Such involvement does not mean that teachers ask questions and wait for children to supply correct answers, nor does it describe a situation in which teachers examine texts prior to their reading to determine where to ask their "well-placed questions" (Barrentine, 1996). We, like Oyler (1996), use the term *interactive* to describe a context in which a teacher genuinely shares, not abandons, authority with the children during the reading of the book. Such sharing can be seen repeatedly in the preceding excerpt. When a child asks "What is a kernel?" a classmate responds comfortably and confidently with an answer; his or her information is seen as contributing to the growing understanding and is enhanced by the teacher's contribution of a scientific term. Later, the teacher acknowledges and commends Annie's "excellent question," suggesting that they continue to read the book to see if the answer will be provided. In Oyler's terms, this context in which children feel comfortable to ask and tell creates a situation in which teachers "gain insight into the connections students are making between the text" (p. 150) and their own experiences, other texts, and their understanding of their world. These turns taken by children provide opportunities for revealing the way texts and information work at the exact moments when children are attempting to reason out new ideas and connections.

Children and their meaning-making efforts are at the center of this process. In the example given, children freely offer comments about the pictures, such as "Look at the bowl!" They ask questions such as "What's a kernel?" and they respond to others' questions, as in "Like what you pop," throughout the reading. These interactive read-alouds not only support co-construction of meaning, but also provide teachers with the opportunity to model expert meaning-making, reasoning, and comprehension processes. In this example, the teacher uses her compliment to signal that Annie has contributed something very important to the current reading-and-understanding effort. Posing questions (and seeking their answers) has long been identified as a significant comprehension strategy (e.g., Dole, Duffy, Roehler, & Pearson, 1991; Pearson & Fielding, 1991; Pearson, Roehler, Dole, & Duffy, 1992; Pressley, Johnson, Symons, McGoldrick, & Kurita, 1989). Although children are at the center, the effort is interactive. The teacher uses Annie's question to model this comprehension strategy for the students: "Let's read and we'll see if this [book] answers that question."

Anne Barry, the classroom teacher who worked with Oyler and Pappas (Oyler, 1996; Oyler & Barry, 1996; Pappas & Barry, 1997), noted that for her, interactive read-alouds allowed her to know how her students approached meaning-making tasks, which thus provided insights into the students' cognition. This information allowed her to better support, scaffold, and extend her students' initiations as they reasoned their way through ideas presented in their text, and as a class, they co-constructed knowledge on particular topics as the class did in the preceding example involving *The Popcorn Book*. This type of scaffolding, modeling reading strategies, supporting risk taking, and sharing control by teachers has been found to produce greater gains in work with students in special education than were made by the students of teachers who spent their time evaluating responses or dominating the instructional conversation (Englert, Tarrant, Mariage, & Oxer, 1994; Mariage, 1995).

Information Books

Previously, we explained why we focus on the information book instead of the more traditionally studied storybook. The information book has many features that make it an excellent genre for initiating and engaging children in interactive read-alouds. It expands world knowledge as new information and concepts are presented, frequently in far greater depth than in subject-area textbooks. These introductions to new vocabulary and concepts are the impetus for children's spontaneous questions, reflections, and connections, as well as teachers' decisions to model, scaffold, or direct attention to certain aspects, information, or connections. As shown in the preceding example, children ask questions about new vocabulary—"What's a kernel?"—and speculate about new concepts on the basis of their prior knowledge, such as when Annie wondered, "What if you, like, would you think [of] a popcorn seed? Like a popcorn seed. Could you grow popcorn?"

Information books also have a greater likelihood of introducing students to grammatical constructions and complex text structures specific to nonfiction texts (Martin & Rothery, 1986; Pappas, 1991, 1993) and necessary for communicating information in society (e.g., Kress, 1994; Martin, 1989). Knowledge of these linguistic features is particularly important given the French study in which researchers (Demont & Gombert, 1996) found that syntactic knowledge was a better predictor of reading comprehension than phonological awareness was for the children in these researchers' 4-year follow-up study. Exposure to the complex text structures of nonfiction texts is also provided during these read-alouds. Just as posing questions and seeking their answers has long been acknowledged as an important comprehension strategy, so, too, has been an awareness of text structure. Knowledge of these global structures supports children's comprehension by providing them with frameworks, or schemas, for anticipating the organizational patterns of the information (e.g., Pearson et al., 1992; Pressley et al., 1989).

Informational texts may also be more likely to hold boys' and struggling readers' attention (Caswell & Duke, 1998; Donovan, Smolkin, & Lomax, 2000). Caswell and Duke (1998) found that information books captured and held the attention of two boys (both struggling readers) during an after-school reading clinic and served as a "catalyst for literacy development" (p. 108). Our work (Donovan et al., 2000; Smolkin, Donovan, & Lomax, 2000) shows boys to be particularly interested in information books, which was demonstrated by the large numbers of self-selections of this genre and their enthusiastic discussions of these selections with their peers.

Teacher Awareness of Important Features

To create interactive contexts such as we presented, teachers must develop a number of domains in their content knowledge. They must be aware of the variety and range of information trade books that are available. They must also grow in their understanding of the different types and levels of inferences that may be necessary for children to comprehend a given passage. They must also be able to discern places in the text that might prove difficult for children.

Each year, more and more information trade books become available. Teachers must become familiar with these texts to use them effectively to add depth to both their curriculum and their interactive read-alouds. As with children, the more teachers use and discuss information books, the more familiar teachers will become with the common text structures and linguistic features of these books (see Donovan & Smolkin, 2002, for an in-depth examination of these genre features). Text complications (when the text fails to support readers) occur for many reasons in informational texts, including the author's assumptions of background knowledge, too much or too little explanation of a new concept, and lack of cohesion among ideas presented. Familiarizing themselves with the books before reading them aloud will help teachers anticipate places where children might have questions. Teachers will also be able to consider where connections might be made with curricular studies, with individual students' interests, and with general prior knowledge as a way to enhance understanding, and where such connections may be necessary to support understanding of complex or dense information. However, this type of perusal is different from the extensive preplanning that is required by some strategy instruction (e.g., *Questioning the Author*; Beck, McKeown, Hamilton, & Kucan, 1997) that depends on teachers asking all the "well-placed" questions.

Time for In-Depth Reading Experiences

Finally, successful interactive information book read-alouds require adequate time for in-depth readings of the books. Although information book readings do not necessitate the beginning-to-end reading sequence of a storybook, time for reading must allow for discussion of the new ideas that are presented, as they are presented. An interactive read-aloud cannot occur without sufficient time to read the book and to have the conversations that happen along the way. Without attention to time, teachers have no way to suggest to students that we can "see if this [book] answers that question" and if it does not, to have time to "talk about it at the end."

van den Broek and Kremer (2000) noted time for in-depth processing of texts as a feature of programs that are effective in improving reading comprehension performance. They noted that in programs such as reciprocal teaching (Palincsar & Brown, 1984) and peer-assisted learning strategies (Fuchs & Fuchs, 2000), "it is quite common to devote an entire class hour to understanding a few paragraphs" (van den Broek & Kremer, 2000, p. 21). The interactive information book read-alouds that we describe in this article were delivered not to provide intensive comprehension instruction (a point we made previously), but rather to allow children access to a world of ideas beyond their first-grade reading ability. Entire books were read in sessions that ranged from 15 min to 30 min.

In the preceding discussion, we delineated the rationale behind the notion of comprehension acquisition and the key features of the interactive information book read-aloud. We next turn our attention to the possible place of these precomprehension strategy instruction ideas in a curriculum designed to enhance the knowledge and affective domains of students in special education classes.

WATERING UP A CURRICULUM

Ellis and Wortham (1999) described the limitations of particular types of adaptations that seem prevalent in content-area instruction in special education practice. These accommodations in task and content often result in situations in which students in special education are confronted with the following:

- A simplified, but disjointed, curriculum of concepts and facts.
- Reduced numbers of opportunities to learn.
- Reduced opportunities to develop thinking skills.
- Less comprehensible texts in which critical cohesive factors have been eliminated to lower calculated readability.
- Reduced intrinsic motivation to learn.

These minimized components result in what Ellis and Wortham termed a watered-down curriculum. To counter such an experience for students in special education, Ellis and Wortham suggested, what is needed is a *watered-up* curriculum that will "facilitat[e] meaningful learning and develop … deep knowledge structures to create 'thought-full' classrooms for students with learning disabilities" (p. 144). The goals of such a watered-up curriculum address both the knowledge domain and the affective domain of student learning.

Placing the Interactive Information Book Read-Aloud Within a Watered-Up Curriculum

Although our research on the interactive information book read-aloud was conducted with first graders and not adolescents, we present examples from our data to demonstrate various aspects of both the knowledge domain and the affective domain of student learning that can be achieved by nonreaders and struggling readers. Regarding the goals of the knowledge dimension, interactive information book read-alouds support "more emphasis on students constructing knowledge"; "more depth, less superficial coverage"; "more emphasis on developing relational understanding and knowledge connections to real-world contexts"; "more student elaboration"; and "more emphasis on developing effective habits of the mind" (Ellis & Wortham, 1999, p. 144). To show all this, we present four excerpts from classroom read-alouds, which we discuss in terms of the watering-up domains represented within them.

Listening in on The Popcorn Book.   In the following example, the teacher (Carol) and her students have finished reading de Paola's (1978) *The Popcorn Book.* They have checked to make sure that they have answered the question that we presented previously when Annie wondered whether popcorn was a seed that could be planted. This question leads the children to further discussion about popcorn, plants, and plans.

Child 1:   You could plant that?

Carol: Yes, you can. Yes, you can.

Child 2:   Is that like at Rowlands [a local garden center]?

Carol: No. You don't have to go to a seed store. You can buy it, get it, in the bag. So, I want everyone to go home and if you have some, get a couple of seeds and put a baggy with some wet paper towels—

Child 3:   Can we do an experiment to see, um, like ask our parents at the grocery store to buy us Pop Quiz and plant the—

Child 4:   Maybe we can plant the two different kinds—

Child 3:   color, a color in the garden, or something. And see what color—

Carol: Ahh. So Pop Quiz is colored popcorn kernels?

Child 3:   Yeah, there's green and others.

Carol: Oh. That would be a good experiment. You ought to do that.... And you could give a report on it.

Child 5:   Maybe we could do the two different kinds—like Pop Quiz and regular popcorn—and see which one of them grows.

From a watering-up perspective, this example clearly shows children constructing knowledge. They are checking to make sure that they understand that popcorn is a seed, a real seed, like seeds that they have seen their families purchase at a garden center. Not only are they constructing this knowledge, but they are also moving a step beyond to applying their knowledge. They interrupt their teacher's suggestion for an experiment, forwarding their own ideas.

They are also involved in "developing relational understanding and knowledge connections to real-world contexts" (Ellis & Wortham, 1999, p. 144); their teacher supports them in this aspect throughout this reading. A child asks, "Maybe, when it comes off and it's really sunny and hot, maybe it pops?" Her teacher responds, "You think so? If we just laid one on the sidewalk you think it might?" This read-aloud allows children to think back to their previous experiences, to consider as one of the children suggests that "sometimes when it's popping and you have the lid on, sometimes the popcorn is stronger than the lid and it pops the lid back...off."

Student elaboration, another knowledge dimension in a watered-up curriculum, is obvious in the few remarks shared thus far. Our transcript for this read-aloud shows how child after child brings prior experience to the reading.

The watering-up knowledge dimension of "more emphasis on developing effective habits of the mind" (Ellis & Wortham, 1999, p. 144) is also being built through this interactive read-aloud. What is notable in this excerpt is the comfort with which the children in this classroom discuss experiments. Their teacher's attitude toward different forms of knowledge construction ("So, I want everyone to go home and…get a couple of seeds and put a baggy with some wet paper towels—") is reflected immediately as children suggest their own questions and methods for answering them.

Listening in on A Chick Hatches.   A reading of Cole and Wexler's (1976, p. 28) *A Chick Hatches* demonstrates how information trade books supply in-depth, rather than superficial, coverage of topics.

> Child: That yellow stuff wasn't there. [Why did it disappear?]
>
> Carol: Well, it might have dried up, or it might be a little bigger. Let's keep reading and see. <u>Inside the membrane, the fetus looks more and more like a chick. Notice how much of the yolk has been used up. Every day now until hatching some of the yolk will be drawn into the chick's body.</u>
>
> Child: Why?
>
> Child: Why? Does he eat the egg?
>
> Child: Oh, gross!
>
> Carol: Well, remember, remember the blood vessels are in the yolk and they get the food from the yolk, so yeah, it uses it up. He doesn't eat it with his mouth, but he eats it through his blood vessels.
>
> Child (whispering):   Wow!

This excerpt clearly demonstrates how reading information books not only supplies considerable depth of information, but also engages the affective domain. Children's affect is clear—they are eager to know the why and how of the yolk's disappearance ("Why?" "Why? Does he eat the egg?"); they are appalled to think of a certain way this might occur ("Oh, gross!"); they are amazed at how the chick actually consumes the yolk ("Wow!").

In terms of a watered-up curriculum that attends to students' affective domains, little doubt exists that these children are engaged in "reflection, risk taking and active participation" (Ellis & Wortham, 1999, p. 144). As we noted previously, informational texts are of great interest to students.

Listening in on Sunken Treasure.   In the following example, the teacher has been reading aloud from Gail Gibbons's (1988) *Sunken Treasure*. The text that prompts student efforts at constructing their own understanding as knowledge is as follows:

Wind ripped at the Atocha's sails, spraying water on top of the deck. Two hundred sixty-five people aboard ship are terrified. Suddenly a huge wave lifts the ship and throws it against a reef. The hull breaks open and the Atocha, along with several of its sister ships, sinks beneath the waves.

Teacher (pointing to picture): See what happened to it?

Child 1: It happened! [The ship has struck the reef.]

Child 2: It looks like—

Teacher: Yes, it really did [happen]; this is a true story about this ship "The Atocha."

Child 3: Ooooh—reef. What's a reef?

Teacher: A reef is like—

Child 4: A mountain.

Teacher: A reef is like a line of rocks. They smashed into.... Like these were rocks and it smashed into the side of the rocks.

Child 5: Rocks...

Carol: [That] is a reef.

Child 6: Like it was really really close and ran into it.

Carol: See it here?

Child 7: I am gonna bring my car and see what happens when I throw it against the rocks.

Regarding the development of relational understanding and connections to real-world contexts, this example shows students actively constructing the relationships among a ship, a reef, and the drowning of the ship's inhabitants. A child's vocabulary question "What's a reef?" elicits a possible answer from a peer and a more definitive answer from the teacher. Although the teacher helps to define the term, the children continue working out the specifics of the crash—the ship must have gotten too close. However, just getting close does not satisfy another child. He suggests that he can provide an opportunity for the class to see what actually happens when an object is thrown against the rocks. Not only does this read-aloud offer an opportunity for the group to construct an understanding around the text, but it also prompts a child to plan an event after the conclusion of this school-based reading. Linking their reading to their real-world knowledge occurs repeatedly for children as they read these information texts in a context in which their teacher supports their contributions.

Listening in on Tree Trunk Traffic. If White (1996), Krashen (1976, 1981), and Salomon and Perkins (1989) were correct, effective habits of the mind, higher order thinking, and information-processing skills are acquired during interactions with more knowledgeable "others." In the next segment, the teacher is reading from Bianca Lavies's (1989) *Tree Trunk Traffic*.

Teacher: Insects live on the tree, too. This big cicada just crawled out of its brown, shell-like skin. For several years— (*The teacher pauses. The next word in the text is* it.) Let's start back here. Insects live on the tree, too. This big cicada just crawled out of its brown, shell-like skin.

Child (interrupting):   We already read this.

Teacher: I know, but see, sometimes if you stop, it helps [to reread the previous sentences]. It didn't make sense just reading [further in the text].

We (Smolkin & Donovan, 2001) have noted this excerpt to be of particular interest. The teacher stops because the referent for the upcoming pronoun is not the skin, as we would expect, but the cicada itself. Working through this momentary interruption, the teacher says, "Let's start back here." The children protest; they want to get on with the book. In response, their teacher indicates that sometimes, in reading, something might not make sense. In this case, a helpful strategy—one in which she immediately engaged—is to reread to reestablish coherence.

What is important in this instance is that student comments, a key in the interactive aspect, result in an adult's making visible what we are to do when acts of comprehension go awry. In this case, children without strong reading skills are being introduced to both effective habits of the mind and solid information-processing skills. If texts do not make sense, we must stop our reading and repair our acts of comprehension.

Limitations of the Interactive Information Book Read-Aloud in a Watered-Up Curriculum

Our particular precomprehension instruction approach supports considerable growth in knowledge domains, but students themselves are not reading. Because of that, this approach may be unable to deliver the powerful sense of personal achievement or potency obtained when students realize that they or their peers have used taught strategies to gain an understanding of text. Neither does this particular approach afford opportunities for developing social responsibility, another goal of a watered-up curriculum (Ellis & Wortham, 1999, p. 144). These achievements must wait until students are able to read texts and participate not just in comprehension acquisition but in structured comprehension instruction.

IMPLICATIONS FOR PRACTICE

The interactive information book read-aloud is best used to serve a particular period (comprehension acquisition) and a particular population (emerging readers, nonreaders, and struggling readers). We believe that the read-aloud should be considered in light of the need to provide rich contexts for engaging children in meaning-making processes, the processes that will be necessary when children begin to read texts on their own. These kinds of experiences can provide for children's continuing comprehension acquisition until they become able to benefit from comprehension strategy instruction. Although the research presented in this article focused on first graders, our most recent investigations included children through fifth grade who were identified by their teachers as struggling readers and who were participating in an after-school reading program. Initial analyses of these data indicate that third- through fifth-grade struggling readers respond with interest and enthusiasm to information book read-alouds with patterns of interactions similar to those of the first graders discussed in this article. Given these preliminary analyses, we suggest that interactive information book read-alouds be considered and experimented with in all educational settings with struggling readers and nonreaders so that they too may learn to reason with informational texts.

FUTURE RESEARCH

There is still much to be learned about comprehension acquisition of nonreaders. We need to examine the place of interactive information book read-alouds in reading instruction for older students who have struggled for years with reading fluency, but have not been identified with learning disabilities. We need to understand whether read-alouds of such texts will strengthen the content knowledge of older students and aid them in compensating for slower decoding rates. We need research examining whether this implicit instruction may, in fact, benefit struggling readers' measured comprehension and their ability to reason through difficult texts. Ultimately, we need research that explores a continuum of school-based comprehension activities, locating the appropriate times and amounts of both implicit and explicit comprehension instruction.

REFERENCES

Adams, B. C., Bell, L. C., & Perfetti, C. A. (1995). A trading relationship between reading skill and domain knowledge in children's text comprehension. *Discourse Processes, 20,* 307–323.

Barrentine, S. J. (1996). Engaging with reading through interactive read-alouds. *Reading Teacher, 50,* 36–43.

Beck, I. L., McKeown, M. G., Hamilton, R. L., & Kucan, L. (1997). *Questioning the author: An approach for enhancing student engagement with text.* Newark, DE: International Reading Association.

Caswell, L. J., & Duke, N. K. (1998). Non-narrative as a catalyst for literacy development. *Language Arts, 75,* 108–117.

Cole, J., & Wexler, J. (1976). *A chick hatches.* New York: Morrow.

Demont, E., & Gombert, J. E. (1996). Phonological awareness as a predictor of recoding skills and syntactic awareness as a predictor of comprehension skills. *British Journal of Educational Psychology, 66,* 315–332.

de Paola, T. (1978). *The popcorn book.* New York: Holiday House.

Dickinson, D. K., & Smith, M. W. (1994). Long-term effects of preschool teachers' book readings on low-income children's vocabulary and story comprehension. *Reading Research Quarterly, 29,* 104–122.

Dole, J. A., Duffy, G. G., Roehler, L. R., & Pearson, P. D. (1991). Moving from the old to the new: Research on reading comprehension instruction. *Review of Educational Research, 61,* 239–264.

Donovan, C. A., & Smolkin, L. B. (2002). Considering genre, content, and visual features in the selection of trade books for science instruction. *Reading Teacher, 55,* 502–520.

Donovan, C. A., Smolkin, L. B., & Lomax, R. G. (2000). Beyond the independent-level text: Readability of first graders self-selections. *Reading Psychology, 21,* 309–333.

Duke, N. K. (2000). 3.6 minutes per day: The scarcity of informational texts in first grade. *Reading Research Quarterly, 35,* 202–224.

Ellis, E. S. (1989). A model for assessing cognitive reading strategies. *Academic Therapy, 24,* 407–424.

Ellis, E. S., & Wortham, J. F. (1998). "Watering up" content instruction. In W. N. Bender (Ed.), *Professional issues in learning disabilities: Practical strategies and relevant research findings* (pp. 141–186). Austin, TX: PRO-ED.

Englert, C. S., Tarrant, K. L., Mariage, T. V., & Oxer, T. (1994). Lesson talk as the work of reading groups: The effectiveness of two interventions. *Journal of Learning Disabilities, 27,* 165–185.

Fuchs, L. S., & Fuchs, D. (2000). Building student capacity to work productively during peer-assisted reading activities. In B. M. Taylor, M. F. Graves, & P. van den Broek (Eds.), *Reading for meaning: Fostering comprehension in the middle grades* (pp. 95–115). New York: Teachers College Press.

Gibbons, G. (1988). *Sunken treasure.* New York: Harper Trophy.

Juel, C., & Leavell, J. A. (1988). Retention and nonretention of at-risk readers in first grade and their subsequent reading achievement. *Journal of Learning Disabilities, 21,* 571–580.

Krashen, S. (1976). Formal and informal linguistic environments in language acquisition and language learning. *TESOL Quarterly, 10,* 157–168.

Krashen, S. (1981). *Second language acquisition and second language learning.* Oxford, England: Pergamon.

Kress, G. (1994). *Learning to write* (2nd ed.). New York: Routledge.

Lavies, B. (1989). *Tree trunk traffic.* New York: Dutton.

Mariage, T. V. (1995). Why students learn: The nature of teacher talk during reading. *Learning Disability Quarterly, 18,* 214–234.

Martin, J. R. (1989). *Factual writing: Exploring and challenging social reality.* Oxford, England: Oxford University Press.

Martin, J. R., & Rothery, J. (1986). What a functional approach to the writing task can show teachers about "good writing." In B. Couture (Ed.), *Functional approaches to writing: Research perspectives* (pp. 241–265). Norwood, NJ: Ablex.

Morrison, F. J., Griffith, E. M., & Frazier, J. A. (1996). Schooling and the 5 to 7 shift: A natural experiment. In A. J. Sameroff & M. Haith (Eds.), *The five to seven year shift: The age of reason and responsibility* (The John D. and Catherine T. MacArthur Foundation series on mental health and development, pp. 161–186). Chicago: University of Chicago Press.

Oyler, C. (1996). Sharing authority: Student initiations during teacher-led read-alouds of information books. *Teaching and Teacher Education, 12,* 149–160.

Oyler, C., & Barry, A. (1996). Intertextual connections in read-alouds of information books. *Language Arts, 73,* 324–329.

Palincsar, A. S., & Brown, A. L. (1984). Reciprocal teaching of comprehension fostering and comprehension-monitoring activities. *Cognition and Instruction, 1,* 117–175.

Pappas, C. C. (1991). Fostering full access to literacy by including information books. *Language Arts, 68,* 449–461.

Pappas, C. C. (1993). Is narrative "primary"? Some insights from kindergartners' pretend readings of stories and information books. *Journal of Reading Behavior, 25,* 97–129.

Pappas, C. C., & Barry, A. (1997). Scaffolding urban students' initiations: Transactions in reading information books in the reading aloud curriculum genre. In N. J. Karolides (Ed.), *Reader response in elementary classrooms* (pp. 215–236). Mahwah, NJ: Lawrence Erlbaum Associates, Inc.

Pearson, P. D., & Fielding, L. (1991). Comprehension instruction. In R. Barr, M. L. Kamil, P. Mosenthal, & P. D. Pearson (Eds.), *Handbook of reading research* (Vol. 2, pp. 815–860). New York: Longman.

Pearson, P. D., Roehler, L. R., Dole, J. A., & Duffy, G. G. (1992). Developing expertise in reading comprehension. In S. J. Samuels & A. E. Farstrup (Eds.), *What research has to say about reading instruction* (pp. 145–199). Newark, DE: International Reading Association.

Perfetti, C. A. (1985). *Reading ability.* New York: Oxford University Press.

Pressley, M., Johnson, C. J., Symons, S., McGoldrick, J. A., & Kurita, J. A. (1989). Strategies that improve children's memory and comprehension of text. *Elementary School Journal, 90,* 3–32.

Salomon, G., & Perkins, D. N. (1989). Rocky roads to transfer: Rethinking mechanisms of a neglected phenomenon. *Educational Psychologist, 24,* 113–142.

Smolkin, L. B., & Donovan, C. A. (2001). The contexts of comprehension: The information book read aloud, comprehension acquisition, and comprehension instruction in a first-grade classroom. *Elementary School Journal, 102,* 97–122.

Smolkin, L. B., & Donovan, C. A. (2002). "Oh, excellent, excellent question!": Developmental differences and comprehension acquisition. In C. Collins-Block & M. Pressley (Eds.), *Comprehension instruction: Research-based best practices* (pp. 140–157). New York: Guilford.

Smolkin, L. B., Donovan, C. A., & Lomax, R. G. (2000). Is narrative primary? Well, it depends…. *National Reading Conference Yearbook, 49,* 511–520.

Stanovich, K. E. (1991). Word recognition: Changing perspectives. In R. Barr, M. L. Kamil, P. Mosenthal, & P. D. Pearson (Eds.), *Handbook of reading research* (Vol. 2, pp. 418–452). New York: Longman.

van den Broek, P., & Kremer, K. E. (2000). The mind in action: What it means to comprehend during reading. In B. M. Taylor, M. F. Graves, & P. van den Broek (Eds.), *Reading for meaning: Fostering comprehension in the middle grades* (pp. 1–31). New York: Teachers College Press.

White, S. H. (1996). The child's entry into the age of reason. In A. J. Sameroff & M. Haith (Eds.), *The five to seven year shift: The age of reason and responsibility* (The John D. and Catherine T. MacArthur Foundation series on mental health and development, pp. 18–30). Chicago: University of Chicago Press.

EXCEPTIONALITY, *11*(1), 39–60

Structuring Instruction to Promote Self-Regulated Learning by Adolescents and Adults With Learning Disabilities

Deborah L. Butler

Department of Educational and Counselling Psychology and Special Education
University of British Columbia

When alternative models for teaching strategies for academic tasks such as reading, studying, writing, and math are compared, certain common pedagogical activities stand out as central to effective instruction. For example, in empirically validated models, instruction is contextualized in meaningful work, long term, explicit, and interactive. At the same time, in devising models, researchers draw on different theoretical assumptions to justify instructional practices, and, correspondingly, the models vary in the degree to which direct instruction of strategies is emphasized. In this article, I describe 1 strategies-training model—strategic content learning (SCL)—that integrates cognitive-behavioral, sociocultural, and constructivist learning theories as a way to shift focus away from the direct instruction of predefined strategies. The article begins with a description of the theoretical rationale for SCL. This description is followed by a review of research documenting SCL efficacy for postsecondary students with learning disabilities. Next, a naturalistic, multi-school study at the secondary level is described, and preliminary findings are outlined. Finally, conclusions focus on defining theoretical issues in need of further research.

When alternative models for teaching strategies to students for key academic tasks such as reading, studying, writing, and math are compared, certain common pedagogical activities stand out as central to effective instruction. For example, in empirically validated models, instruction is contextualized in meaningful work, long term, explicit, and interactive (e.g., see Ellis, 1993; Harris & Graham, 1996; Palincsar & Brown, 1988; Pressley et al., 1992). However, in creating models, researchers draw on varying theoretical assumptions about teaching and learning associated with instructional practices, and, correspondingly, the models vary in the degree to which direct instruction of task-specific strategies is emphasized (Butler, 1998b; Pressley et al., 1995; Pressley, Snyder, & Carglia-Bull, 1987).

Requests for reprints should be sent to Deborah L. Butler, Department of Educational and Counselling Psychology and Special Education, Faculty of Education, University of British Columbia, Vancouver, BC V6T 1Z4, Canada. E-mail: deborah.butler@ubc.ca

In this article, I highlight the theoretical assumptions underlying various approaches to strategy training, with the ultimate goal of providing an integrative framework for understanding instructional features.

The strategic content learning (SCL) approach (Butler, 1993, 1995, 1998c), founded on an integration of cognitive-behavioral, sociocultural, and constructivist learning theories, provides an excellent contrast to intervention models wherein direct instruction and modeling of predefined strategies are central (e.g., Borkowski & Muthukrishna, 1992; Ellis, 1993; Schumaker & Deshler, 1992). This article begins with an overview of various approaches to strategy training and the theoretical principles on which they are based. This overview is followed by a description of the rationale for SCL and a review of research documenting SCL efficacy for postsecondary students with learning disabilities (Butler, 1993, 1995, 1998d; Butler, Elaschuk, & Poole, 2000). Next, a naturalistic, multischool study at the secondary level is described, and preliminary findings are outlined. Finally, conclusions focus on defining areas in which further research is needed to clarify the relationship between strategies instruction and desired learning outcomes.

WHAT COUNTS AS STRATEGIES INSTRUCTION?

Gersten and Smith-Johnson (2000) raised the question of what counts as strategy training. They argued that, within strategies instruction, students should learn strategies that are specific and that "break complex cognitive tasks into smaller steps" (p. 172). Further, drawing on Ellis and Lenz's (1987) work, they emphasized that strategies should "consist of brief and simple steps," "employ a remembering system," and "employ cues to implement cognitive strategies, metacognition, and application of rules and to take over action" (Gersten & Smith-Johnson, 2000, p. 172). This description is consistent with the instructional approach that characterized many early approaches to strategy training. Specifically, a teacher or a researcher analyzed a task (e.g., reading or writing) to determine what was required, articulated required cognitive activities as a series of steps, and then taught these steps explicitly to students (in tandem with mnemonic devices). In early models, emerging in the 1970s, methods for teaching strategies focused almost exclusively on direct explanation and modeling, followed by opportunities for guided and independent practice (see Pressley et al., 1987). Teachers and researchers hoped that during and after instruction students would translate the simplified descriptions of cognitive processes (i.e., articulated in strategy steps) into meaningful and situated action, internalize these approaches to learning, and transfer strategy use across contexts.

However, as early as the 1980s, researchers recognized that explicit explanation and modeling of strategy steps alone were insufficient to promote strategic performance (Groteluschen, Borkowski, & Hale, 1990; Pressley et al., 1995). Of concern was the consistent finding that students failed to transfer strategy use across contexts and time (Brown, Campione, & Day, 1981; Wong, 1991b, 1994). As a result, instructional models were elaborated in various ways to address the transfer problem (e.g., Borkowski & Muthukrishna, 1992; Ellis, 1993; Englert, Raphael, Anderson, Anthony, & Stevens,

1991; Harris & Graham, 1996; Palincsar & Brown, 1984, 1988; Pressley et al., 1995; Schumaker & Deshler, 1992). For example, some researchers focused attention on how students' motivational beliefs mediate strategic performance (e.g., Bandura, 1993; Borkowski & Muthukrishna, 1992; Schunk, 1994; Zimmerman, 1989, 1995). Thus, instructional models emerged that promoted positive self-perceptions of control and competence in tandem with knowledge about strategies (e.g., Borkowski, Weyhing, & Carr, 1988). Built from this research, most current strategy-training models incorporate instructional components directly focused on motivation.

Another example of an elaborated model is Ellis's (1993) comprehensive integrative strategies instruction (ISI). In ISI, students are first guided to use effective strategies through a kind of procedural facilitation (i.e., structured cues to guide cognitive processing that mirror strategy steps; see Englert, 1992), before direct explanation about strategies is provided. As a result, students have opportunities to build from rich and contextualized experiences when they are making sense of strategy descriptions, rather than trying to translate simplified descriptions of cognitive processes directly into complex and contextualized action. ISI also includes activities explicitly directed at supporting transfer. For example, in later stages of instruction (once strategies are learned), students are encouraged to "experiment, evaluate, and refine" strategies to meet their individual needs (Ellis, 1993, p. 370).

Many researchers have emphasized the importance of embedding strategy instruction in the context of meaningful work (Ellis, 1993; Harris & Graham, 1996; Palincsar & Brown, 1984, 1988; Palincsar & Klenk, 1992; Pressley et al., 1992). Teaching strategies in context highlights the relevance of strategies and at the same time promotes students' flexible adaptation of strategies given varying task demands. An early model that exemplifies this approach is Palincsar and Brown's (1984) reciprocal teaching. In the original applications of reciprocal teaching, students learned and implemented reading strategies while collaboratively interpreting text (Palincsar & Brown, 1984, 1988).

Finally, in most emerging models, direct instruction and modeling of strategies is extended by providing opportunities for discussion and interaction. In recognition of students' active role in constructing knowledge about tasks, strategies, and themselves as learners (Campione, Brown, & Connell, 1988; Harris & Pressley, 1991; Paris & Byrnes, 1989), students are engaged in activities during which they must use and discuss strategies with others and articulate understandings about learning. Thus, for example, in Palincsar and Brown's (1984, 1988) reciprocal teaching, students work in small groups and read together while applying reading strategies. Students also take turns leading discussions and supporting one anothers' strategic activities. Similarly, in Pressley et al.'s (1992) transactional strategies instruction (TSI), students construct understandings about texts and about reading strategies as they talk together about reading together.

In sum, emerging models for strategies training have become increasingly sophisticated and complex. Although direct instruction about learning strategies remains a mainstay of instruction, models have also incorporated a rich array of instructional practices designed to support students' independent strategic activity. Moreover, consistent with Gersten and Smith-Johnson's (2000) definition of strategies instruction, each retains a focus, to some degree, on directly communicating specific learning strategies comprising a series of simplified steps.

THEORETICAL PRINCIPLES UNDERLYING
STRATEGIES INSTRUCTION

Three theoretical perspectives have converged to ground development of these emerging instructional variants. First, approaches to strategy training have been influenced by cognitive-behavioral learning theories (Dole, Duffy, Roehler, & Pearson, 1991). Consistent with a task-analytic approach to instruction, cognitive activities required for task completion are broken down into a series of steps that, when taught to students, provide rules to guide action in the presence of relevant cues (i.e., task demands). Taken to extremes, this theoretical perspective undergirds Gersten and Smith-Johnson's (2000) equating of strategy training with teaching specific cognitive routines. In contrast, while retaining a focus on direct instruction of strategies, most researchers also draw from cognitive-behavioral theories to emphasize students' active role in self-regulation and self-management (e.g., Zimmerman, 1989, 1994). In fact, central to emerging models is an emphasis on students' roles in self-instruction, self-direction, and self-monitoring (e.g., Butler & Winne, 1995; Harris & Graham, 1996).

Second, other strategy-training researchers have emphasized sociocultural models of teaching and learning when describing learning and teaching processes (e.g., Englert, 1992; Palincsar & Brown, 1984, 1988). Researchers have interpreted Vygotsky's (1978) sociocultural theory as suggesting that students become more strategic when they internalize cognitive processes that are first explained or modeled by others (e.g., Borkowski & Muthukrishna, 1992; Englert, 1992; Palincsar & Brown, 1984). The scaffolding metaphor for instructional processes that is currently so prevalent reflects this underlying perspective. The notion is that instructors construct a scaffold by guiding students' learning activities. Then, once students make externally guided cognitive processes their own, the scaffold is deconstructed. As Borkowski and Muthukrishna (1992) explained, "The ultimate goal of scaffolding is to develop student independence through the gradual internalization of the processes that are encouraged during scaffolded instruction" (p. 491).

A third perspective about teaching and learning that has shaped emerging strategy-training models derives from a constructivist position. In constructivist models, students are described as active learners who construct knowledge on the basis of experience (e.g., Harris & Pressley, 1991; Paris & Byrnes, 1989). Drawing on a constructing metaphor rather than an internalizing metaphor allows us to imagine students building situated knowledge that reflects idiosyncratic, even unanticipated, understandings (Butler, 1998b).

These three theoretical perspectives are reflected simultaneously in many emerging instructional models. For example, models that emphasize direct instruction of strategies and the promotion of self-regulation have their roots in cognitive-behavioral theories. Simultaneously, elaborated models include activities derived from sociocultural or constructivist perspectives. For example, reciprocal teaching includes scaffolded support and external guidance for cognitive processing as students start to use strategies (Campione et al., 1988; Palincsar & Brown, 1984, 1988). Interactive discussions about strategies in the context of meaningful work also foster students' active construction of knowledge as students strive to interpret material and then make sense of their cognitive experiences. In fact, many strategy-training researchers in the 1990s emphasized the dual roles of social and constructive processes in students' development of strategic learning (e.g., Harris & Pressley, 1991;

Stone & Reid, 1994). A combination of all three perspectives (cognitive-behavioral, sociocultural, and constructivist) may be necessary for a multidimensional understanding of complex teaching and learning processes.

At the same time, recognizing how theoretical assumptions have an impact on what are considered necessary instructional processes is important. For example, contrast transmission approaches with teaching science with inquiry-based models based on constructivist principles (e.g., Palincsar, Anderson, & David, 1993). Clearly, cognitive-behavioral and constructivist assumptions can be harnessed to promote very different instructional practices. In the context of strategy training, internalizing and constructing metaphors can create different visions of learning, and thus of essential instructional activities (see Butler, 1998b; Stone, 1998). For example, if the internalizing metaphor is interpreted narrowly, it images students as recipients of cultural knowledge. The implication is that instructors must guide student processing externally first, until students internalize the processes first modeled by others. Similarly, a limited interpretation of cognitive-behavioral principles can lead to a restricted focus on knowledge transmission (in this case, knowledge about strategies). In contrast, constructivist theories describe students as active problem solvers who construct knowledge on the basis of experience, building from what they already know (Butler, 1998b). From a constructivist perspective, critical instructional features might include opportunities for students to engage in active inquiry related to authentic problems or issues as an alternative to direct instruction about particular content or strategies (e.g., Palincsar et al., 1993).

In sum, multiple conceptions of teaching and learning coexist in emerging instructional models. Because instructional principles can be associated with alternative instructional practices, the implications of perspectives that researchers adopt need to be clear. At the same time, each perspective likely contributes uniquely to an understanding of teaching and learning. Thus, developing an integrative understanding across cognitive-behavioral, sociocultural, and constructivist perspectives is key to advancing understanding about how and why strategy instruction might work.

THE SCL APPROACH

SCL (Butler, 1993, 1995) evolved from earlier approaches to strategy training (e.g., Palincsar & Brown, 1984; Pressley et al., 1987). As such, SCL builds on previous research and shares features with other instructional models. For example, as in other instructional models, and consistent with Gersten and Smith-Johnson's (2000) prescription, in SCL, discussions about strategies are specific, systematic, and explicit (Butler, 1999b). Attention also focuses on supporting students' construction of metacognitive knowledge as well as positive self-perceptions of competence (e.g., perceptions of self-efficacy; Bandura, 1993; Schunk, 1994; Wong, 1991a). Further, as in Ellis's (1993) ISI, in SCL, instructors provide a form of procedural facilitation, when necessary, by guiding students to complete learning tasks effectively (through questioning) and then helping them derive generalized understandings about cognitive processes on the basis of these experiences. Finally, as in reciprocal teaching (Campione et al., 1988; Palincsar & Brown, 1984) and TSI (Pressley et al., 1992), SCL instruction engages students in interactive discussions about strategic processing as they engage in meaningful work. However, SCL also differs from other instructional models in certain key respects. One is that direct instruction of predefined strategies is not provided (see Butler, 1993, 1994, 1998b).

Several theoretical arguments converged in the development of SCL to suggest this approach to teaching strategies. In this section, some of these arguments are outlined, both to clarify SCL instructional principles and, in light of the issues raised in preceding sections, to highlight how SCL contributes to an understanding of teaching and learning processes. Throughout this discussion, attention focuses on how SCL integrates principles derived from cognitive-behavioral, sociocultural, and constructivist perspectives. Although other instructional models could be analyzed similarly, attention in this section focuses on instructional principles associated with SCL (and not on a comparison of models). Figure 1 provides a summary of SCL theoretical principles in relation to associated instructional activities.

First, SCL instructional methods emerged from an analysis of strategic performance (Brown, 1980, 1987; Butler & Winne, 1995; Resnick & Glaser, 1976; Schoenfeld, 1988; Wong, 1991a; Zimmerman, 1989). Drawing on a cognitive-behavioral perspective (e.g., Zimmerman, 1989, 1994), models of self-regulated learning suggest that strategic learners engage recursively in a cycle of problem-solving activities—namely, analyzing tasks, implementing task-appropriate strategies, monitoring outcomes associated with strategy use, and adjusting strategies accordingly (Butler & Winne, 1995; Zimmerman, 1989, 1994). From this perspective, promoting strategic learning requires much more than just teaching strategies (Butler, 1999a; Harris & Graham, 1996). Students must also learn how to analyze tasks so as to set criteria for guiding and judging performance. Further, students need to know how to monitor outcomes and how to use this information to redirect learning (Butler & Winne, 1995). Thus, the primary instructional goal in SCL is to promote students' self-regulated learning. To accomplish this objective, teachers facilitate students' movement through cycles of task analysis, strategy development, and monitoring. Within this broader context, students are assisted to learn how to select, adapt, or even invent strategies on the basis of an analysis of task requirements (see Butler, 1993, 1995).

Second, theoretical analysis of the origin of self-regulation also influenced the development of SCL (Butler, 1998b; Butler & Winne, 1995; Flavell, 1987; Vygotsky, 1978). In this context, distinguishing between two subcomponents of self-regulation—metacognitive knowledge and self-regulating processes—is important because each may develop differently (Butler, 1998a). *Metacognitive knowledge* refers to students' knowledge about learning and encompasses knowledge about tasks, strategies, and learners (Brown, 1987; Flavell, 1987). Motivational beliefs, like metacognitive knowledge, also reflect students' metacognitive understanding. For example, students' attributional beliefs reflect their knowledge about causal factors related to successful or unsuccessful performance (Borkowski et al., 1988; Weiner, 1974), whereas students' task-specific perceptions of self-efficacy reflect self-perceptions of competence and control (Bandura, 1993; Schunk, 1994). Many researchers argue that students actively construct metacognitive knowledge and motivational beliefs with time on the basis of successive experiences with tasks (e.g., Harris & Pressley, 1991; Paris & Byrnes, 1989). The depth of students' metacognitive understandings may increase with time as developmental changes foster greater self-reflection and analytic thinking in students (Butler, 1998a).

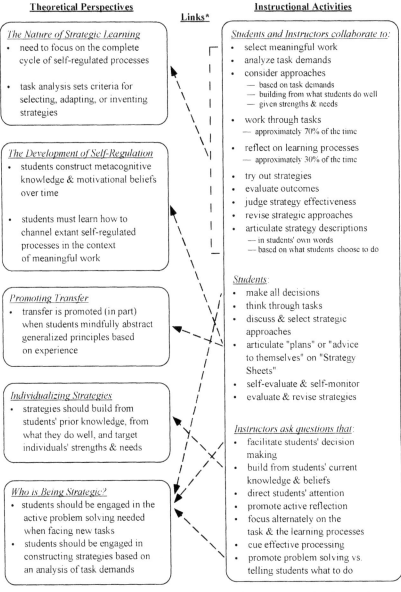

* These are examples of links between principles and practices, not a comprehensive set of connections

FIGURE 1   Theoretical principles underlying strategic content learning instruction and connections to instructional practices.

In terms of students' engagement in the cycle of self-regulating processes, researchers offer varying descriptions of how effective self-regulation develops. For example, one perspective is that students need to be taught how to self-regulate. This view is consistent with transmission approaches to strategy training that seek to communicate strategic repertoires to students (see Butler & Winne, 1995). A second view, alluded to previously, is that students become independently self-regulating by internalizing learning processes that are first observed in social contexts. This perspective, the most common application of sociocultural principles, underlies approaches that start by guiding students' learning processes externally (i.e., through direct instruction, modeling, or procedural facilitators) and then gradually release control as students independently start to self-direct learning (i.e., the move from other- to self-regulation; e.g., Borkowski & Muthukrishna, 1992; Englert, 1992; Palincsar & Brown, 1984). A final perspective is that even young children are self-regulating in their interactions with the world. For example, consider Vygotsky's (1978) description of a preschooler's obtaining an unreachable cookie with the aid of a stick. From this perspective, instruction in self-regulation per se is unnecessary. Rather, students need to learn how to channel strategic efforts effectively when they are faced with new kinds of tasks (Butler, 1995, 1998b) and then how to construct understandings over time regarding their strategic approaches to learning (Butler, 1998a).

In the SCL theoretical model, the hypothesis is that sociocultural and individual forces interact to shape students' construction of self-regulated approaches to academic work, metacognitive knowledge, and motivational beliefs. For example, drawing on Vygotsky's (1978) original writings and on constructivist theories can yield the hypothesis that students do not enter school as self-regulating blank slates (Butler & Winne, 1995) but are inherently self-regulated in their interactions with the environment. Thus, to shape students' strategic approaches to academic work, SCL instructors help students to decipher academic requirements and then to collaboratively problem solve strategic approaches.

Also built from a constructivist perspective is the hypothesis that students construct metacognitive knowledge as they engage self-regulating processes and reflect on their learning experiences (Paris & Byrnes, 1989). At the same time, SCL reflects the recognition that students are strongly influenced by the cultural contexts in which they learn. Social contexts define the materials (i.e., language and tools) that students use to make sense of experience (Butler, 1998b; Stone & Reid, 1994; Wertsch, 1979). Thus, knowledge construction (by students and teachers) is assumed to be socially situated, coconstructed, and emerging from reflective discourse based on meaningful experience (Butler, 1995; Harris & Pressley, 1991; Paris & Byrnes, 1989). Further, the social interaction with instructors or peers facilitates students' coconstruction of "transactional understandings" that are more elaborate and sophisticated than understandings that any individual might construct alone (see Pressley et al., 1992). These transactional coconstructions may contribute to domain-specific knowledge (e.g., as when students coconstruct transactional understandings about text while reading collaboratively; Pressley et al., 1992) or to students' development of metacognitive knowledge about tasks, strategies, or their respective learning processes. Following these assumptions, SCL instructors engage students in interactive discussions focused alternately on task completion and on the process of completing a task. Within social interactions, students coconstruct better approaches to learning, metacognitive knowledge, and motivational beliefs, all of which are shaped within social and cultural contexts.

A third influence on SCL instructional principles is derived from an analysis of learning mechanisms associated with transfer (e.g., Salomon & Perkins, 1989; Wong, 1991b, 1994). Consistent with a constructivist perspective, one conclusion from this analysis is that transfer is supported, in part, when students approach tasks reflectively, or "mindfully," and abstract generalized principles about learning on the basis of concrete task experiences (Salomon & Perkins, 1989; Wong, 1994). Thus, in SCL, students are not initially required to make sense of learning principles abstracted by teachers or researchers into a sequence of predefined strategy steps. Instead, students are guided to self-regulate performance successfully and then to abstract generalized principles about learning that build from prior knowledge and are formulated in their own words.

A fourth question that drove the development of SCL centered on how strategy instruction could be individualized. Although students with learning disabilities encounter some common difficulties (e.g., decoding words or building comprehension while reading), they nonetheless have multidimensional cognitive profiles along with varying experiences, strengths, and needs (Pintrich, Anderman, & Klobucar, 1994). Thus, strategies that work well for one student may not be effective for another (Montague, 1993; Swanson, 1990). Further, all but the youngest students have a budding knowledge base about strategies for accomplishing academic tasks. As a result, approaches that teach the same strategies to all students, without accounting for prior knowledge, may not be maximally efficient (Butler, 1994, 1995). Thus, SCL was designed to afford opportunities for students to construct personalized strategies that build from what they do well and respond to their individual needs.

A final theoretical argument underlying SCL emerged from evaluating who it is that is strategic in some approaches to strategy training. In some cases, the teacher or the researcher is the person who considers an academic task, identifies associated goals, considers the types of problems that students might encounter, and defines a specific and, it is hoped, effective routine. This routine is conveyed directly to the students. However, in this scenario, students are essentially excluded from the problem-solving process that is at the heart of strategic learning (Butler & Winne, 1995). Students do not necessarily learn how to confront a novel task, identify goals, and brainstorm, try out, and modify various approaches designed to meet task requirements. Thus, SCL students are engaged in the process of defining strategic alternatives, given task goals. The expectation is that students will learn to recognize that they, too, can generate strategic approaches and ultimately control learning outcomes.

In sum, multiple theoretical strands converged to shape SCL instructional principles. As a result, SCL situates strategy instruction in the broader enterprise of promoting self-regulation, fosters students' mindful construction of knowledge about learning processes, and engages students in collaborative problem solving during which they construct individualized strategies that are built from prior knowledge and responsive to how they learn best. Unlike instructional models that emphasize direct instruction, no predefined learning strategies are described in SCL. Instead, instructors provide calibrated support to students—using guiding questions—that assists them to self-regulate learning and to develop more effective strategies in that context. Figure 1 facilitates understanding of how SCL instructional principles are translated into practice by providing an overview of instructional procedures.

A SUMMARY OF SCL RESEARCH AT THE
POSTSECONDARY LEVEL

To date, seven intensive intervention studies have been completed that evaluate SCL efficacy for students with learning disabilities in college or university settings. In each study, a common research design was used. First, to trace the relationship between instructional activities and students' development of self-regulation, researchers collected in-depth case study data for each participant (Merriam, 1998; Yin, 1994). At the same time, multiple case studies were embedded within a pre–post design. During pretest and posttest sessions, parallel questionnaires, observations, and interviews were used to measure common effects among students (see Butler, 1993, 1995, 1998d).

Across the seven studies, SCL was adapted for use in the three most common service delivery models used in colleges and universities. In four studies (n = 35), SCL was implemented as a model for individualized tutoring by learning specialists, counselors, or teachers (see Butler, 1993, 1995, 1998c, 1998d). In another two studies (n = 14), SCL served as a model for peer tutor training (see Butler, Elaschuk, Poole, MacLeod, & Syer, 1997). The seventh study (n = 21) investigated SCL adapted for use within small-group discussions as part of a study skills course (see Butler, Elaschuk, Poole, Novak, et al., 2000). Thus, across studies, 70 postsecondary students participated in interventions in which they received support following the SCL model.

Psychoeducational assessments verified that each participant had a learning disability, although students' specific learning disabilities affected different aspects of their performance. Further, many students experienced concomitant disabilities that also affected their learning (e.g., a visual impairment or attention deficit disorder). Participants were enrolled in a broad range of programs. Some of these programs focused on basic academic upgrading (e.g., for math at the fifth-grade level). Other students were enrolled in vocational (e.g., in early childhood education, medical lab technician, or diesel mechanics), academic (e.g., university transfer, first-year university courses), or professional (e.g., law, education) programs. This diversity facilitated evaluating the robustness of the SCL model across students, settings, programs, and tasks.

In postsecondary settings, SCL support was provided as an adjunct to regular classroom instruction. In the individualized tutoring and peer tutor studies, students chose the tasks that they wanted to work on (typically variants of reading, writing, studying, and math tasks), and the assignments were drawn from individuals' programs of study. In the group-based study skills course, small groups worked primarily on either reading and studying or writing, but task examples were drawn from participants' actual work. At each meeting, students prioritized assignments on the basis of current course requirements, and SCL tutors provided calibrated assistance as students self-regulated completion of these tasks. In all studies, instructors met with students (as individuals or in small groups) two to three times a week (for 2–4 hr per week) during at least a single semester. Information on participant age, gender, and participation in SCL interventions (i.e., number of intervention sessions, total time involved) is presented in Table 1.

In each study, instructors began by supporting students to analyze task requirements, articulate performance criteria, and set specific goals. At this (and every other) stage of instruction, support targeted individuals' needs. For example, if a student held misconceptions about a task, the instructor supported the student to scrutinize task descriptions or assignment exemplars to abstract more accurate conceptions. Next, instructors supported students to select, adapt, or even invent strategies in light of task goals. Instead of teaching preidentified strategies, instructors assisted students to problem solve strategies by building from strategies they already knew. Doing so often entailed asking students to implement current strategies, monitor outcomes associated with strategy use, and maintain, revise, or replace strategies on the basis of discrepancies between progress and goals. When students' current strategies were clearly inadequate, students and instructors brainstormed alternatives and evaluated options (given task demands). Both students and instructors contributed suggestions to this discussion, but students ultimately were asked to take responsibility for making decisions about which strategies to use.

Finally, instructors observed students' strategic performance and supported their cognitive processing "online." When obstacles were encountered or at natural breaks in the task, students were encouraged to reflect on their performance, to self-evaluate progress, and to make judgments about how to proceed. As in strategy selection, task

TABLE 1
Overview of Participants Across the Seven Postsecondary Studies (1993–1999)

Study	n^a	Media Age (Min–Max)	Gender		Median No. Intervention Sessions (Min–Max)	Median Total Time Spent (hr)[b] (Min–Max)
			Male	Female		
SCL 1993	8	26.00 (18–36)	3	5	10.50 (7–15)	15.50 (11.00–28.50)
SCL 1994	13	32.00 (21–45)	3	10	14.00 (8–20.50)	18.25 (8.50–25.75)
Innovations years studies, 1 & 2	14	32.00 (19–48)	5	9	18.50 (9–39)	18.75 (11.50–43.50)
Peer tutor projects (2)	14	24.50 (19–49)	8	6	8.00 (2–24)	9.75 (2.50–24.50)
Group study	21	32.00 (19–55)	10	11	13.00 (5–19)	20.00 (7.50–28.25)
Total	70	29.50 (18–55)	29	41	13.75 (2–39)	17.25 (2.50–43.50)

Note.   SCL = strategic content learning.
[a]A number of students participated in two consecutive studies. In these totals, the students are counted only once (so they underestimate the number of students per study). Data from these students included their age at the beginning of the first study and the average number of sessions and time spent across the two studies.
[b]rounded to the nearest one-quarter hour.

criteria set the standards against which progress toward learning goals was judged (Butler & Winne, 1995). Thus, within each intervention session, students were assisted to diagnose problems (cognitive, motivational, or volitional; Corno, 1993), to build on what they already did well, and to revise strategies that were not working. With time, students were assisted to build personalized strategies based on their unique processing strengths and weaknesses and in response to their particular difficulties with tasks. Through this process, students were assisted to construct not only better task-specific strategies, but also metacognitive and volitional strategies for managing learning activities (Butler, 1998a; Corno, 1993, 1994).

Analyses of outcome data across the seven studies suggested that, in general, SCL intervention at the postsecondary level is associated with improvement in students' task performance; metacognitive knowledge about tasks, strategies, and self-monitoring; perceptions of self-efficacy (Bandura, 1993; Schunk, 1994); and patterns of attributions (Borkowski & Muthukrishna, 1992; Weiner, 1974). Students developed personalized strategies that addressed their individual needs. They were also observed to take an active role in strategy development and to transfer strategic performance across contexts and tasks (see Butler, 1993, 1995, 1998d; Butler, Elaschuk, Poole, Novak, et al., 2000). A summary of findings from the subset of data related to changes in task performance, metacognitive knowledge, and motivational beliefs is presented in Table 2. This table presents a set of columns that summarize statistically reliable gains across studies (indicated with an asterisk). Columns 2 through 4 summarize outcomes from four studies in which SCL was used as a model for individualized tutoring by learning specialists, counselors, or teachers (see Butler, 1993, 1995, 1998d). Column 5 depicts pooled results from two studies wherein peer tutors were trained to use SCL (see Butler et al., 1997). The final column presents the results from a study in which SCL was used in a group-based study skills course (see Butler, Elaschuk, Poole, Novak, et al., 2000).

The results reported in Table 2, coupled with the findings summarized previously (e.g., improvements in task performance and self-regulated processing), suggest, first, that SCL instruction can be associated with significant gains across several types of outcomes. This finding is particularly notable given that these gains were achieved in a relatively short period by students with long-standing difficulties. Second, the most consistent and powerful gains were achieved by students who received individualized tutoring from learning specialists, counselors, or teachers (see columns 2–4), although students in the group-based study skills courses also appeared to make substantial improvements (see column 6). Finally, results from the two peer tutor studies were more limited. Close scrutiny of the data from the peer-tutoring projects showed that when tutors faithfully implemented the SCL approach, tutees made clear gains (see Butler et al., 1997). However, general effects appeared to be diluted as a result of logistical and administrative barriers (e.g., hiring peer tutors halfway through the semester; difficulties coordinating training for tutors). Additional research is planned to assess SCL efficacy as a model for peer tutor training when these barriers are removed.

Given the evidence for SCL efficacy for students at the postsecondary level, additional analyses were conducted to trace how SCL works (e.g., Duffy, Roehler, & Rackliffe, 1986; Gaskins, Anderson, Pressley, Cunicelli, & Satlow, 1993; Mehan, 1985). For example, in one study (Kamann & Butler, 1996), a discourse analysis was completed to

TABLE 2
Summary of Postsecondary Outcomes: Significant Pretest-to-Posttest Comparisons

| Measure | Significant Effects by Study[a] | | | | |
	SCL 1993	SCL 1994	Innovations Studies	Peer Tutor Studies	Group Study
Task performance	*	*	*	n/a	*
Metacognitive knowledge[b]					
Task description	n/a	*	*	—	*
Strategy description	n/a	*	*	—	*
Strategy focus	n/a	*	*	—	*
Monitoring	n/a	*	*	*	—
Overall (average)	*	*	*	—	*
Self-efficacy					
Global self-efficacy	n/a	—	—	—	—
Task-specific confidence	n/a	*	*	—	*
Perceived competence	*	*	*	*	*
Task preference	*	—	n/a	n/a	n/a
Ability rating	*	*	—	—	—
On targeted task	n/a	*	*	*	*
On other academic tasks	n/a	—	*	*	*
Attributions					
Successful performance					
Ability	*	—	*	—	—
Effort	*	—	—	—	—
Strategy use	*	—	*	—	*
Depended on others	—	—	*	—	—
Unsuccessful performance					
Ability	*	*	—	—	—
Effort	—	—	—	—	—
Strategy use	—	—	—	—	—
Depended on others	*	—	—	—	—

Note. * = results that were statistically reliable; — = results that were not statistically reliable; n/a = not assessed in this study.
[a]SCL 1993 ($n = 8$), see Butler (1993, 1995); SCL 1994 ($n = 13$), see Butler (1998c, 1998d); innovations studies, years 1 and 2 pooled ($n = 21$), see Butler (1998c, 1998d); peer tutor studies ($n = 14$–25, depending on criteria for inclusion), see Butler et al. (1997); group study ($n = 21$), see Butler, Poole, et al. (2000). [b]As a way to assess changes in metacognitive dimensions, scores from SCL 1994 and the innovations studies were pooled (see Butler, 1998d).

describe the dynamics of student–instructor interactions during one-on-one tutoring. This analysis documented how strategic performance could be supported through facilitative questioning, without direct instruction and modeling of strategies. In another analysis, in-depth case study data were compared for three students who worked on writing (Butler, Elaschuk, & Poole, 2000). The analysis showed how various positive outcomes could be associated with students' strategy development. Further, the analysis showed how the content of students' strategies was a joint function of the demands of writing tasks (e.g., in terms of planning, drafting text, and revising) and students' individual needs. Finally, another analysis described instructor and peer interactions from the group-based study skills classes (Butler, Elaschuk, Poole, Novak, et al., 2000). In this analysis, my coworkers and I documented how students coconstructed strategies in small-group discussions by trading ideas while they were constructing personalized interpretations of strategies. Taken together, these various analyses illuminate the interplay between social and individual processes in students' development of self-regulation (Stone & Reid, 1994).

ADAPTING SCL IN SECONDARY SCHOOLS

Following the postsecondary studies, a multiyear, multischool project was launched at the secondary level. This project emerged from an in-service presentation for learning assistance teachers. Ten teachers expressed a desire to participate in a districtwide, collaborative study of how SCL could be situated in secondary classrooms. Nine teachers chose to use SCL when they were working in learning assistance or resource settings (for students in Grades 8–11), and one teacher used SCL in a whole classroom setting (with her ninth-grade students). A team of five researchers worked collaboratively with these teachers to define strategies for implementing SCL within varying school and classroom cultures and to evaluate benefits for teachers and students.

A summary of findings from the first year of the project is provided next. These findings reflect only a subset of analyses because the project is still underway. Much of the first year was spent developing, implementing, monitoring, and revising systems for situating SCL in classrooms. In fact, one goal of the study has been to evaluate the kinds of collaborative professional development activities that promote meaningful instructional change (Borko & Putnam, 1998; Butler, Novak, Beckingham, Jarvis, & Elaschuk, 2001; Palincsar, 1999; Perry, Walton, & Calder, 1999). Although this longer term development effort was necessary, both to provide time for meaningful collaboration to occur and to define useful strategies for contextualizing SCL, the result was that many students were not consistently engaged in SCL instruction until well into the school year. A more effective test of SCL efficacy came from the second year of the project, wherein SCL implementation was effected more quickly, in part because sample classroom routines were available for both new ($n = 4$) and continuing ($n = 7$) teachers. In fact, by the third week of class in the second year, teams of as many as 10 individuals at each school (including teachers, educational assistants, and peer tutors) had already begun to apply the SCL model and had constructed contextualized classroom routines.

Similar to the blended design used in the postsecondary studies, the design of the secondary project involved multiple, parallel, in-depth case studies embedded within a two-group (intervention group and comparison group), pretest–posttest design (see Butler, Elaschuk, Jarvis, Beckingham, & Novak, 2001). Intervention students received SCL instruction from their teachers as part of the natural flow of instruction. Comparison students in five parallel classrooms received a comparable amount of support from teachers who used their typical teaching methods. Observations of intervention and comparison group classrooms were conducted as a way to document instructional processes and evaluate both the extent of SCL implementation in intervention classrooms and the kind of instruction provided to comparison groups. In all learning assistance or resource settings (intervention and comparison classrooms), teachers met with students in small class settings with a ratio of 4 to 7 students per teacher. Students brought coursework to these classes, and teachers circulated among students to provide individualized support. Blocks typically lasted for 70 to 100 min. Two of the four schools were on a semester schedule, so that support blocks met every day. The other two schools were on a year-long schedule, so that support blocks met every 2 days. The teacher who used SCL in her whole classroom also taught at one of the year-long schools. She met with students in a double block for English and humanities courses combined.

As in the postsecondary studies, pretest and posttest questionnaires and interviews assessed students' metacognitive knowledge about tasks and strategies and motivational beliefs (e.g., causal explanations for successful and unsuccessful performance; perceptions of control over outcomes; task-specific perceptions of self-efficacy; Bandura, 1993; Borkowski, 1992; Schunk, 1994; Weiner, 1974). Case study data included copies of students' classroom assignments and tests, copies of the strategies that students developed, and teachers' reflections on instructional processes and observed outcomes for students (recorded in classroom logs). Teachers participated in three all-schools meetings evenly distributed throughout the year, and minutes were maintained from these meetings. Finally, teachers were interviewed at the end of the year, and their perspectives about SCL, collaborative processes, and outcomes were gathered.

Preliminary findings that emerged from data analyses are highlighted next. These analyses included systematic qualitative analyses of minutes from all-schools meetings and transcripts from teachers' exit interviews (see Merriam, 1998; Miles & Huberman, 1994; Yin, 1994), as well as quantitative analyses of some of the pretest–posttest questionnaire data. Overall, findings suggested that students benefited in several ways from participating in SCL intervention. For example, at all-schools meetings and in exit interviews, teachers reported observing gains for students in terms of their (a) independence and self-directedness; (b) self-confidence, pride, and sense of control over learning; and (c) awareness of the value of their individualized learning strategies to their academic success. Preliminary analyses of questionnaire data provided converging evidence for these observations. For example, comparisons of intervention students ($n = 56$) and comparison group students ($n = 17$) in learning assistance or resource settings showed that, after pretest scores were accounted for, intervention students' posttest perceptions of control over outcomes were significantly higher than those of students in the comparison group, Wilks's $F(4, 63) = 2.86$, $p < .05$. Intervention students were more likely to say that they could control outcomes through effort, $F(1, 66) = 5.63$, $p < .05$, or by using strategies, $F(1, 66) = 4.18$, $p < .05$. A significant interaction effect, $F(1, 70) = 4.85$, $p < .05$, elaborated these findings. At the beginning of the year, both intervention students and comparison students were relatively positive that they could control outcomes (average ratings of about 3.5 of 5). However, by the end of the first year (when exams were looming), the perceptions of intervention students remained positive, whereas the perceptions of comparison students declined. No significant group differences or interaction effects were found in students' scores on the self-efficacy scales, which was contrary to expectations. However, significant interactions were also found in analyses based on the attributional data. Again, although intervention students showed positive shifts in attributional patterns from pretest to posttest, the attributional patterns of comparison students deteriorated.

Finally, students' responses to the metacognitive questionnaire were coded along three dimensions, each on a scale from 0 to 3 (see Butler, 1995; Wong, Wong, & Blenkinsop, 1989). These dimensions were (a) task description (students' description of the demands of tasks such as reading, writing, or math), (b) task quality (students' descriptions of criteria for judging performance quality), and (c) strategy description (the clarity of students' descriptions of task-specific strategies). Results from three univariate 2 (group) × 2 (test time) analyses of variance revealed patterns similar to those found in the motivational data. Specifically, for two of the three dimensions (task description and strategy description), scores for intervention students increased between pre- and posttesting, whereas scores for comparison students decreased. This interaction effect was statistically reliable for the strategy description dimension, $F(1, 70) = 4.5$, $p < .04$, and very close to significant for students' task descriptions, $F(1, 70) = 3.675$, $p < .06$. Thus, overall, participation in classes structured according to SCL principles could be associated with positive changes for students in their metacognitive knowledge and motivational beliefs, even in the first year of the study. Additional analyses are underway to identify potentially mediating variables (e.g., class type, school schedule, gender, and grade) and to evaluate outcomes across various other variables (e.g., task performance, strategy transfer). A full set of analyses from the secondary study, along with complementary case study descriptions, are available elsewhere (Butler & Briard, 2000; Butler, Elaschuk, Jarvis, et al., 2001).

That teachers associated the intervention with positive outcomes for students and enjoyed being part of the study was evident in discussions and observations. For example, when the teachers were asked whether they would recommend the intervention approach to colleagues, every teacher ($n = 10$) said "yes." One teacher responded, "Absolutely. There are too many kids who are spoon fed the information and we need to turn them into independent thinkers. I think this is just a marvelous way of doing it." Their actions were consistent with these statements. For example, teachers recommended the intervention to colleagues, two teachers joined the project midyear, and all teachers expressed a willingness to be part of the project again in the second year.

Teachers also believed that SCL was generally useful and should be used with students across subjects and contexts. As one resource teacher explained, "[SCL could be used] in any kind of classroom in any subject area, because we cover all those subjects down here and we used it effectively in every subject area. A classroom teacher could use it." At the same time, teachers identified factors that reduced some students' responsiveness to the approach. For example, one teacher cautioned, "You won't attain the same level of success with every student.... Some kids will buy into it right away. Some will take longer, or they aren't going to get there at all. You have to accept that." Some of the students who did not do as well were struggling with behavioral, personal, health, or emotional challenges. Teachers described other students as resistant to thinking for themselves after a long history of being told what to do. The teachers thought that these students took longer to accept the changed approach and found it frustrating at first. In contrast, students did well when they were willing to slow down to think about strategies and then observe how their progress improved as a result.

In addition to citing positive outcomes for students, teachers identified personal benefits that they achieved from participating in the project: (a) personal satisfaction from observing student improvement (Ball, 1995); (b) positive opportunities to collaboratively problem solve with students, rather than having to be the "expert" all the time; and most significant, (c) shifts in instructional style and understandings about instructional principles (Perry et al., 1999). For example, one teacher noted that she gained 'a totally different perspective of how to teach to students who you would think are lazy. They're not lazy. They're stuck." Another positive shift was that early in the year teachers were afraid to take the time necessary to talk to students about learning processes because they felt obligated to help students complete pressing work. In contrast, by year-end, teachers described the importance of slowing down and helping students proactively problem solve strategies, rather than putting out fires in each class (i.e., crisis management). The teachers also described how they were better able to target their attention to students who really needed help, because students started work independently and were more focused on their studies. Finally, teachers noted that because they really listened to students while they were facilitating learning (in contrast to directly instructing), they were better able to recognize misconceptions, appreciate individual differences, and help students identify personalized strategies. As one teacher explained, "I'm so used to teaching math using the strategies that I have, but I found that students were independently developing strategies that worked better for them" (Ball, 1995).

CONCLUSION

The results overviewed in this article suggest that SCL provides a viable model for supporting postsecondary students with learning disabilities across varying service delivery structures. College and university participants in the SCL studies experienced multifaceted and positive outcomes, including improvement in task performance; metacognitive knowledge about tasks, strategies, and monitoring; perceptions of self-efficacy; and attributions for academic performance (Butler, 1993, 1995, 1998c, 1998d; Butler, Elaschuk, Poole, Novak, et al., 2000). Students were also observed to be actively involved in strategy development and to transfer strategy use across contexts and tasks. Taken together, these results suggest that students not only learned effective task-specific strategies, but also learned how to self-regulate performance across a range of tasks. Similarly, preliminary findings from the first year of the SCL secondary study are encouraging, although additional research is required to thoroughly validate SCL in that context.

On the basis of the theoretical analysis provided in this article, several other areas were identified that require additional research. For example, one question centers on whether direct instruction of specific strategies is a necessary component of strategy training, as Gersten and Smith-Johnson (2000) argued. Although many successful strategy-training interventions incorporate direct instruction as part of a multidimensional instructional program, the success of the SCL intervention suggests that direct instruction is not always essential. Nevertheless, explicit and systematic discussion about strategies is a feature shared across empirically validated models (e.g., Butler, 1993, 1995; Ellis, 1993; Englert, 1992; Harris & Graham, 1996; Palincsar & Brown, 1984, 1988; Pressley et al., 1992; Schumaker & Deshler, 1992). Additional research is required to tease apart the relative contributions of varying instructional activities for students at different ages and different levels.

Another important avenue to explore more fully is the nature of calibrated support. In calibrated support, teachers typically guide students' cognitive processing responsively, building from individuals' current understandings. This key concept is subsumed within the scaffolding instructional metaphor so prevalent across instructional models. However, descriptions of students' internalizing predefined processes may not adequately capture the richness of students' learning experiences. A fuller understanding of instruction–learning relationships might be better captured by integrating sociocultural and constructivist perspectives.

Another critical research direction is to define how strategies instruction fits within the broader enterprise of developing capable learners. Although not always framed in terms of self-regulated processes, most effective instructional models explicitly promote task understanding, adaptive strategy selection, and monitoring, in addition to strategy mastery (e.g., Butler, 1995; Ellis, 1993; Englert, 1992; Harris & Graham, 1996; Palincsar & Brown, 1984). SCL provides another example of how instruction can be structured to promote problem solving and strategic learning rather than simple strategy mastery.

Finally, common activities across many instructional models are those that engage students in active inquiry, collaborative problem solving, and interactive discussions about learning. Within these types of activities, students have opportunities to actively construct personalized understandings that are shaped by sociocultural processes. However, because the joint implications of constructivist and sociocultural theories are only now being appreciated (e.g., Butler, 1998b; Harris & Pressley, 1991; Paris & Byrnes, 1989; Stone & Reid, 1994), further inquiry is required to define how self-regulation is promoted in the content of collaborative and interactive discussions and to uncover the relative roles of social and individual processes in students' development of metacognition, motivation, and self-regulating processes.

ACKNOWLEDGMENTS

This research was supported in part by a Social Sciences and Humanities Research Council of Canada Standard Research Grant. I thank the members of my research team, including Cory Elaschuk, Shannon Poole, Helen Novak, Sandra Jarvis, and Beverly Beckingham, for their assistance across the various projects described in this article. I also thank Vicki Rothstein, Denise Briard, Karen Vendyback, Sharon Sall, Suzanne Meyburgh, Maryam Naser, Debra Forestier, Sandra Loren, Dione Holmes, Brenda Dewonck, Lisa Pauls, Joan Richter, and Gina Rae for their participation in the secondary project. Finally, I am grateful to Ed Ellis for his insightful feedback on earlier drafts of this article.

REFERENCES

Ball, D. L. (1995). Blurring the boundaries of research and practice. *Remedial and Special Education, 16*, 354–363.

Bandura, A. (1993). Perceived self-efficacy in cognitive development and functioning. *Educational Psychologist, 28*, 117–148.

Borko, H., & Putnam, R. (1998). Professional development and reform-based teaching: Introduction to the theme issue. *Teaching and Teacher Education, 14,* 1–3.

Borkowski, J. G. (1992). Metacognitive theory: A framework for teaching literacy, writing, and math skills. *Journal of Learning Disabilities, 25,* 253–257.

Borkowski, J. G., & Muthukrishna, N. (1992). Moving metacognition into the classroom: "Working models" and effective strategy teaching. In M. Pressley, K. R. Harris, & J. T. Guthrie (Eds.), *Promoting academic competence and literacy in school* (pp. 477–501). Toronto: Academic.

Borkowski, J. G., Weyhing, R. S., & Carr, M. (1988). Effects of attributional retraining on strategy-based reading comprehension in learning-disabled students. *Journal of Educational Psychology, 80,* 46–53.

Brown, A. L. (1980). Metacognitive development and reading. In R. J. Spiro, B. C. Bruce, & W. F. Brewer (Eds.), *Theoretical issues in reading comprehension: Perspectives from cognitive psychology, linguistics, artificial intelligence, and education* (pp. 453–481). Hillsdale, NJ: Lawrence Erlbaum Associates, Inc.

Brown, A. L. (1987). Metacognition, executive control, self-regulation, and other more mysterious mechanisms. In F. E. Weinert & R. H. Kluwe (Eds.), *Metacognition, motivation, and understanding* (pp. 65–116). Hillsdale, NJ: Lawrence Erlbaum Associates, Inc.

Brown, A. L., Campione, J. C., & Day, J. D. (1981). Learning to learn: On training students to learn from texts. *Educational Researcher, 10*(2), 14–21.

Butler, D. L. (1993). *Promoting strategic learning by adults with learning disabilities: An alternative approach.* Unpublished doctoral dissertation, Simon Fraser University, Burnaby, British Columbia, Canada.

Butler, D. L. (1994). From learning strategies to strategic learning: Promoting self-regulated learning by post secondary students with learning disabilities. *Canadian Journal of Special Education, 4,* 69–101.

Butler, D. L. (1995). Promoting strategic learning by post secondary students with learning disabilities. *Journal of Learning Disabilities, 28,* 170–190.

Butler, D. L. (1998a). Metacognition and learning disabilities. In B. Y. L. Wong (Ed.), *Learning about learning disabilities* (2nd ed., pp. 277–307). Toronto: Academic.

Butler, D. L. (1998b). In search of the architect of learning: A commentary on scaffolding as a metaphor for instructional interactions. *Journal of Learning Disabilities, 31,* 374–385.

Butler, D. L. (1998c). A strategic content learning approach to promoting self-regulated learning. In B. J. Zimmerman & D. Schunk (Eds.), *Developing self-regulated learning: From teaching to self-reflective practice* (pp. 160–183). New York: Guilford.

Butler, D. L. (1998d). The strategic content learning approach to promoting self-regulated learning: A summary of three studies. *Journal of Educational Psychology, 90,* 682–697.

Butler, D. L. (1999a, April). *Identifying and remediating students' inefficient approaches to tasks.* Paper presented at the annual meeting of the American Educational Research Association, Montreal, Quebec, Canada.

Butler, D. L. (1999b, April). *The importance of explicit writing instruction for postsecondary students with learning disabilities.* Paper presented at the annual meeting of the Council for Exceptional Children, Charlotte, NC.

Butler, D. L., & Briard, D. (2000). *Promoting independent and strategic learning by adolescents with learning disabilities.* Paper presented at the annual meeting of the Council for Learning Disabilities, Austin, TX.

Butler, D. L., Elaschuk, C. L., Jarvis, S., Beckingham, B., & Novak, H. (2001, April). *Teachers as facilitators of students' strategic performance: Promoting academic success by secondary students with learning difficulties.* Paper presented at the annual meeting of the American Educational Research Association, Seattle, WA.

Butler, D. L., Elaschuk, C. L., & Poole, S. (2000). Promoting strategic writing by postsecondary students with learning disabilities: A report of three case studies. *Learning Disability Quarterly, 23,* 196–213.

Butler, D. L., Elaschuk, C., Poole, S., MacLeod, W. B., & Syer, K. (1997, June). *Teaching peer tutors to support strategic learning by post-secondary students with learning disabilities.* Paper presented at the annual meeting of the Canadian Society for Studies in Education, St. John's, Newfoundland, Canada.

Butler, D. L., Elaschuk, C. L., Poole, S. L., Novak, H. J., Jarvis, S., & Beckingham, B. (2000, April). *Investigating an application of strategic content learning: Promoting strategy development in group contexts.* Paper presented at the annual meeting of the American Educational Research Association, New Orleans, LA.

Butler, D. L., Novak, H., Beckingham, B., Jarvis, S., & Elaschuk, C. L. (2001, April). *Professional development and meaningful change: Towards sustaining an instructional innovation.* Paper presented at the annual meeting of the American Educational Research Association, Seattle, WA.

Butler, D. L., & Winne, P. H. (1995). Feedback and self-regulated learning: A theoretical synthesis. *Review of Educational Research, 65,* 245–281.

Campione, J. C., Brown, A. L., & Connell, M. L. (1988). Metacognition: On the importance of understanding what you are doing. In R. I. Charles & E. A. Silver (Eds.), *The teaching and assessing of mathematical problem solving* (Vol. 3, pp. 93–114). Hillsdale, NJ: Lawrence Erlbaum Associates, Inc.

Corno, L. (1993). The best laid plans: Modern conceptions of volition and educational research. *Educational Researcher, 22*(2), 14–22.

Corno, L. (1994). Student volition and education: Outcomes, influences, and practices. In D. H. Schunk & B. J. Zimmerman (Eds.), *Self-regulation of learning and performance: Issues and educational applications* (pp. 229–251). Hillsdale, NJ: Lawrence Erlbaum Associates, Inc.

Dole, J. A., Duffy, G. G., Roehler, L. R., & Pearson, P. D. (1991). Moving from the old to the new: Research on reading comprehension instruction. *Review of Educational Research, 61,* 239–264.

Duffy, G. G., Roehler, L. R., & Rackliffe, G. (1986). How teachers' instructional talk influences students' understanding of lesson content. *Elementary School Journal, 87,* 3–16.

Ellis, E. S. (1993). Integrative strategy instruction: A potential model for teaching content area subjects to adolescents with learning disabilities. *Journal of Learning Disabilities, 26,* 358–383, 398.

Ellis, E. S., & Lenz, B. K. (1987). A component analysis of effective learning strategies for LD students. *Learning Disabilities Focus, 2*(2), 94–107.

Englert, C. S. (1992). Writing instruction from a sociocultural perspective: The holistic, dialogic, and social enterprise of writing. *Journal of Learning Disabilities, 25,* 153–172.

Englert, C. S., Raphael, T. E., Anderson, L. M., Anthony, H. M., & Stevens, D. D. (1991). Making strategies and self-talk visible: Writing instruction in regular and special education classrooms. *American Educational Research Journal, 28,* 337–372.

Flavell, J. H. (1987). Speculations about the nature and development of metacognition. In F. E. Weinert & R. H. Kluwe (Eds.), *Metacognition, motivation, and understanding* (pp. 21–64). Hillsdale, NJ: Lawrence Erlbaum Associates, Inc.

Gaskins, I. W., Anderson, R. C., Pressley, M., Cunicelli, E. A., & Satlow, E. (1993). Six teachers' dialogue during cognitive process instruction. *Elementary School Journal, 93,* 277–304.

Gersten, R., & Smith-Johnson, J. (2000). Songs of experience: Commentary on "Dyslexia the invisible" and "Promoting strategic writing by postsecondary students with learning disabilities: A report of three case studies." *Learning Disability Quarterly, 23,* 171–174.

Groteluschen, A. K., Borkowski, J. G., & Hale, C. (1990). Strategy instruction is often insufficient: Addressing the interdependency of executive and attributional processes. In T. Scruggs & B. Y. L. Wong (Eds.), *Intervention research in learning disabilities* (pp. 81–101). New York: Springer-Verlag.

Harris, K. R., & Graham, S. (1996). *Making the writing process work: Strategies for composition and self-regulation.* Cambridge, MA: Brookline.

Harris, K. R., & Pressley, M. (1991). The nature of cognitive strategy instruction: Interactive strategy construction. *Exceptional Children, 57,* 392–404.

Kamann, M. P., & Butler, D. L. (1996, April). *Strategic content learning: An analysis of instructional features.* Paper presented as part of a coordinated symposium at the annual meeting of the American Educational Research Association, New York.

Mehan, H. (1985). The structure of classroom discourse. In T. A. Van Dijk (Ed.), *Handbook of discourse analysis* (pp. 119–131). London: Academic.

Merriam, S. B. (1998). *Qualitative research and case study applications in education.* San Francisco: Jossey-Bass.

Miles, M. B., & Huberman, A. M. (1994). *Qualitative data analysis: An expanded sourcebook* (2nd ed.). Thousand Oaks, CA: Sage.

Montague, M. (1993). Student-centered or strategy-centered instruction: What is our purpose? *Journal of Learning Disabilities, 26,* 433–437.

Palincsar, A. (1999). Response: A community of practice. *Teacher Education and Special Education, 22,* 272–274.

Palincsar, A. S., Anderson, C., & David, Y. M. (1993). Pursuing scientific literacy in the middle grades through collaborative problem solving. *Elementary School Journal, 93,* 643–659.

Palincsar, A. S., & Brown, A. L. (1984). Reciprocal teaching of comprehension-fostering and comprehension monitoring activities. *Cognition and Instruction, 1,* 117–175.

Palincsar, A. S., & Brown, A. L. (1988). Teaching and practicing thinking skills to promote comprehension in the context of group problem solving. *Remedial and Special Education, 9*, 53–59.

Palincsar, A. S., & Klenk, L. (1992). Fostering literacy learning in supportive contexts. *Journal of Learning Disabilities, 25*, 211–225, 229.

Paris, S. G., & Byrnes, J. P. (1989). The constructivist approach to self-regulation and learning in the class-room. In B. J. Zimmerman & D. H. Schunk (Eds.), *Self-regulated learning and academic achievement: Theory, research, and practice.* New York: Springer-Verlag.

Perry, N. E., Walton, C., & Calder, K. (1999). Teachers developing assessments of early literacy: A community of practice project. *Teacher Education and Special Education, 22*, 218–233.

Pintrich, P. R., Anderman, E. M., & Klobucar, C. (1994). Intraindividual differences in motivation and cognition in students with and without learning disabilities. *Journal of Learning Disabilities, 27*, 360–370.

Pressley, M., El-Dinary, P. B., Brown, R., Schuder, T., Bergman, J. L., York, M., et al. (1995). A transactional strategies instruction Christmas carol. In A. McKeough, J. Lupart, & A. Martini (Eds.), *Teaching for transfer: Fostering generalization in learning.* Mahwah, NJ: Lawrence Erlbaum Associates, Inc.

Pressley, M., El-Dinary, P. B., Gaskins, I. W., Schuder, T., Bergman, J. L., Almasi, J., et al. (1992). Beyond direct explanation: Transactional instruction of reading comprehension strategies. *Elementary School Journal, 92*, 513–555.

Pressley, M., Snyder, B. L., & Carglia-Bull, T. (1987). How can good strategy use be taught to children? Evaluation of six alternative approaches. In S. M. Cormier & J. D. Hagman (Eds.), *Transfer of learning: Contemporary research and applications* (pp. 81–119). Toronto: Academic.

Resnick, L. B., & Glaser, R. (1976). Problem solving and intelligence. In L. B. Resnick (Ed.), *The nature of intelligence* (pp. 205–230). Hillsdale, NJ: Lawrence Erlbaum Associates, Inc.

Salomon, G., & Perkins, D. N. (1989). Rocky roads to transfer: Rethinking mechanisms of a neglected phenomenon. *Educational Psychologist, 24*, 113–142.

Schoenfeld, A. H. (1988). Problem solving in context(s). In R. I. Charles & E. A. Silver (Eds.), *The teaching and assessing of mathematical problem solving* (Vol. 3, pp. 82–92). Hillsdale, NJ: Lawrence Erlbaum Associates, Inc.

Schumaker, J. B., & Deshler, D. D. (1992). Validation of learning strategy interventions for students with learning disabilities: Results of a programmatic research effort. In B. Y. L. Wong (Ed.), *Contemporary intervention research in learning disabilities: An international perspective* (pp. 22–46). New York: Springer-Verlag.

Schunk, D. H. (1994). Self-regulation of self-efficacy and attributions in academic settings. In D. H. Schunk & B. J. Zimmerman (Eds.), *Self-regulation of learning and performance: Issues and educational applications* (pp. 75–99). Hillsdale, NJ: Lawrence Erlbaum Associates, Inc.

Stone, C. A. (1998). The metaphor of scaffolding: Its utility for the field of learning disabilities. *Journal of Learning Disabilities, 31*, 344–364.

Stone, C. A., & Reid, D. K. (1994). Social and individual forces in learning: Implications for instruction of children with learning difficulties. *Learning Disability Quarterly, 17*, 72–86.

Swanson, H. L. (1990). Instruction derived from the strategy deficit model: Overview of principles and procedures. In T. Scruggs & B. Y. L. Wong (Eds.), *Intervention research in learning disabilities* (pp. 34–65). New York: Springer-Verlag.

Vygotsky, L. S. (1978). *Mind in society.* Cambridge, MA: Harvard University Press.

Weiner, B. (1974). An attributional interpretation of expectancy-value theory. In B. Weiner (Ed.), *Cognitive views of human motivation* (pp. 51–69). New York: Academic.

Wertsch, J. V. (1979). From social interaction to higher psychological processes: A clarification and application of Vygotsky's theory. *Human Development, 22*, 1–22.

Wong, B. Y. L. (1991a). The relevance of metacognition to learning disabilities. In B. Y. L. Wong (Ed.), *Learning about learning disabilities* (pp. 231–258). San Diego, CA: Academic.

Wong, B. Y. L. (1991b, August). *On the thorny issue of transfer in learning disabilities interventions: Towards a three-prong solution.* Invited address, Fourth European Conference for Research on Learning and Instruction, University of Turku, Turku, Finland.

Wong, B. Y. L. (1994). Instructional parameters promoting transfer of learned strategies in students with learning disabilities. *Learning Disability Quarterly, 17*, 110–120.

Wong, B. Y. L., Wong, R., & Blenkinsop, J. (1989). Cognitive and metacognitive aspects of learning disabled adolescents composing problems. *Learning Disability Quarterly, 12,* 300–322.

Yin, R. K. (1994). *Case study research: Design and methods* (2nd ed.). Thousand Oaks, CA: Sage.

Zimmerman, B. J. (1989). A social-cognitive view of self-regulated learning. *Journal of Educational Psychology, 81,* 329–339.

Zimmerman, B. J. (1994). Dimensions of academic self-regulation: A conceptual framework for education. In D. H. Schunk & B. J. Zimmerman (Eds.), *Self-regulation of learning and performance: Issues and educational applications* (pp. 3–21). Hillsdale, NJ: Lawrence Erlbaum Associates, Inc.

Zimmerman, B. J. (1995). Self-regulation involves more than metacognition: A social cognitive perspective. *Educational Psychologist, 30,* 217–221.

www.ingramcontent.com/pod-product-compliance
Ingram Content Group UK Ltd.
Pitfield, Milton Keynes, MK11 3LW, UK
UKHW020427010325
455677UK00029B/1032